MW01141930

WORD 97
VISUAL SOLUTIONS

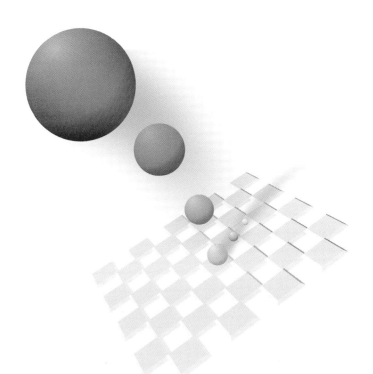

by: maranGraphics' Development Group

Corporate Sales

Contact maranGraphics
Phone: (905) 890-3300
　　　 (800) 469-6616
Fax:　 (905) 890-9434

Canadian Trade Sales

Contact Prentice Hall Canada
Phone: (416) 293-3621
　　　 (800) 567-3800
Fax:　 (416) 299-2529

Visit our Web site at:
http://www.maran.com

Word 97 Visual Solutions

Copyright©   1997 by maranGraphics Inc.
               5755 Coopers Avenue
               Mississauga, Ontario, Canada
               L4Z 1R9

Canadian Cataloguing in Publication Data
Maran, Ruth, 1970-
    Word 97 : visual solutions

(Visual solutions)
Written by Ruth Maran, Kelleigh J. Wing.
Includes index.
ISBN 1-896283-35-7

1. Microsoft Word for Windows (Computer file). 2. Word Processing.
I. Wing, Kelleigh J., 1970-   II. MaranGraphics' Development Group.
III. Title.   IV. Series.

Z52.5.M523M383 1997   652.5'5369   C97-932333-9

Printed in the United States of America

10   9   8   7   6   5   4   3   2   1

All rights reserved. No part of this publication may be used,
reproduced or transmitted, in any form or by any means, electronic,
mechanical, photocopying, recording or otherwise, or stored in any
retrieval system of any nature, without the prior written permission
of the copyright holder, application for which shall be made to:
maranGraphics Inc., 5755 Coopers Avenue, Mississauga, Ontario,
Canada, L4Z 1R9.
This publication is sold with the understanding that neither
maranGraphics Inc., nor its dealers or distributors, warrants the
contents of the publication, either expressly or impliedly, and, without
limiting the generality of the foregoing, no warranty either express
or implied is made regarding this publication's quality, performance,
salability, capacity, suitability or fitness with respect to any specific or
general function, purpose or application. Neither maranGraphics Inc.,
nor its dealers or distributors shall be liable to the purchaser or any
other person or entity in any shape, manner or form whatsoever
regarding liability, loss or damage caused or alleged to be caused
directly or indirectly by this publication.
maranGraphics has used their best efforts in preparing this book. As
Web sites are constantly changing, some of the Web site addresses
in this book may have moved or no longer exist.
maranGraphics does not accept responsibility nor liability for losses
or damages resulting from the information contained in this book.
maranGraphics also does not support the views expressed in the
Web sites contained in this book.

Trademark Acknowledgments

maranGraphics Inc. has attempted to include trademark information
for products, services and companies referred to in this guide.
Although maranGraphics Inc. has made reasonable efforts in
gathering this information, it cannot guarantee its accuracy.

All other brand names and product names used in this book
are trademarks, registered trademarks, or trade names of their
respective holders. maranGraphics Inc. is not associated with
any product or vendor mentioned in this book.

**FOR PURPOSES OF ILLUSTRATING THE CONCEPTS AND
TECHNIQUES DESCRIBED IN THIS BOOK, THE AUTHOR HAS
CREATED VARIOUS NAMES, COMPANY NAMES, MAILING
ADDRESSES, E-MAIL ADDRESSES AND PHONE NUMBERS,
ALL OF WHICH ARE FICTITIOUS. ANY RESEMBLANCE OF
THESE FICTITIOUS NAMES, COMPANY NAMES, MAILING
ADDRESSES, E-MAIL ADDRESSES AND PHONE NUMBERS TO
ANY ACTUAL PERSON, COMPANY AND/OR ORGANIZATION IS
UNINTENTIONAL AND PURELY COINCIDENTAL.**

©1997 maranGraphics, Inc.

The 3-D illustrations are the
copyright of maranGraphics, Inc.

WORD 97

VISUAL SOLUTIONS

VISUAL SERIES 3D

maranGraphics™

Every maranGraphics book represents
the extraordinary vision and commitment of a unique family:
the Maran family of Toronto, Canada.

Back Row (from left to right):   Sherry Maran, Rob Maran, Richard Maran,
Maxine Maran, Jill Maran.

Front Row (from left to right):   Judy Maran, Ruth Maran.

Richard Maran is the company founder and its inspirational leader. He developed maranGraphics' proprietary communication technology called "visual grammar." This book is built on that technology—empowering readers with the easiest and quickest way to learn about computers.

Ruth Maran is the Author and Architect—a role Richard established that now bears Ruth's distinctive touch. She creates the words and visual structure that are the basis for the books.

Judy Maran is the Project Coordinator. She works with Ruth, Richard and the highly talented maranGraphics illustrators, designers and editors to transform Ruth's material into its final form.

Rob Maran is the Technical and Production Specialist. He makes sure the state-of-the-art technology used to create these books always performs as it should.

Sherry Maran manages the Reception, Order Desk and any number of areas that require immediate attention and a helping hand.

Jill Maran is a jack-of-all-trades and dynamo who fills in anywhere she's needed anytime she's back from university.

Maxine Maran is the Business Manager and family sage. She maintains order in the business and family—and keeps everything running smoothly.

CREDITS

Authors:
Ruth Maran and
Kelleigh Wing

**Copy Development, Editing
and Screen Captures:**
Tina Veltri

Project Coordinator:
Judy Maran

Editors:
Brad Hilderley
Raquel Scott
Jason M. Brown
Sandra Hawryn

Layout Designer:
Jamie Bell

Illustrators:
Chris K.C. Leung
Russell C. Marini
Ben Lee
Treena Lees
Peter Grecco

Illustrator & Screen Artist:
Jeff Jones

Indexers:
Kelleigh Wing
Tina Veltri

Post Production:
Robert Maran

ACKNOWLEDGMENTS

Thanks to the dedicated staff of maranGraphics, including
Jamie Bell, Jason M. Brown, Francisco Ferreira, Peter Grecco,
Sandra Hawryn, Brad Hilderley, Jeff Jones, Wanda Lawrie,
Ben Lee, Treena Lees, Peter Lejcar, Chris K.C. Leung,
Michael W. MacDonald, Jill Maran, Judy Maran, Maxine Maran,
Robert Maran, Sherry Maran, Russell C. Marini, Raquel Scott,
Roxanne Van Damme, Tina Veltri, Paul Whitehead and
Kelleigh Wing.

Finally, to Richard Maran who originated the easy-to-use
graphic format of this guide. Thank you for your inspiration
and guidance.

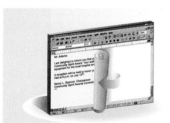

TABLE OF CONTENTS

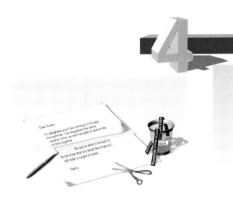

7 FORMAT PARAGRAPHS

8 FORMAT PAGES

TABLE OF CONTENTS

13   WORK WITH GRAPHICS

14   TIME-SAVING FEATURES

15   MAIL MERGE

TABLE OF CONTENTS

16 WORD AND THE INTERNET

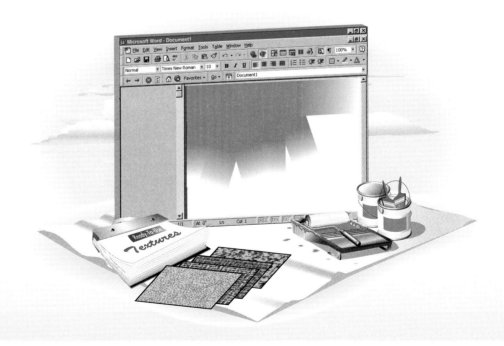

CHAPTER 1

Getting Started

Do you want to begin using Microsoft Word 97? This chapter will help you get started.

Word lets you produce professional-looking documents quickly and efficiently.

You can use Word to create letters, reports, manuals, newsletters and brochures.

Editing

Word offers many features that help you work with text in a document. You can easily edit text, rearrange paragraphs and check for spelling mistakes.

Formatting

You can easily change the appearance of a document. You can add page numbers, center text and use various fonts in a document.

Printing

You can produce a paper copy of a Word document. Word lets you see on the screen exactly what the printed document will look like.

Tables

You can create tables to neatly display information in your document. Word lets you draw a table on the screen as you would draw a table with a pen and paper.

Graphics

Word comes with many types of graphics that you can use to enhance the appearance of your documents.

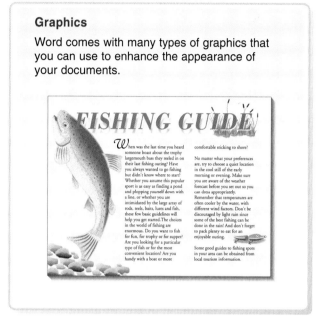

Mail Merge

You can quickly produce personalized letters and mailing labels for each person on a mailing list.

The Internet

You can make documents you create available on the company intranet or the World Wide Web. Word offers many features that help you take advantage of the Internet.

USING THE MOUSE

A mouse is a hand-held device that lets you select and move items on your screen.

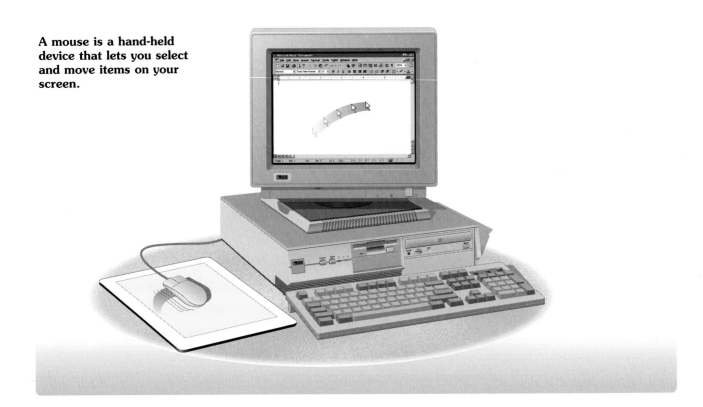

Holding the Mouse

Resting your hand on the mouse, use your thumb and two rightmost fingers to move the mouse on your desk. Use your two remaining fingers to press the mouse buttons.

Moving the Mouse

When you move the mouse on your desk, the mouse pointer on the screen moves in the same direction.

The mouse pointer assumes different shapes (examples: ⌖ or I), depending on its location on the screen and the task you are performing.

Cleaning the Mouse

A ball under the mouse senses movement. You should occasionally remove and clean this ball to ensure smooth motion of the mouse.

MOUSE ACTIONS

Click

Press and release the left
mouse button.

Double-Click

Quickly press and release
the left mouse button twice.

Drag and Drop

Position the mouse pointer (⬚)
over an object on your screen
and then press and hold down
the left mouse button.
Still holding down
the mouse
button, move
the mouse to
where you want
to place the object
and then release the mouse button.

MICROSOFT INTELLIMOUSE

The new Microsoft IntelliMouse
has a wheel between the left and
right mouse buttons. Moving this
wheel lets you quickly scroll
through information on the
screen.

You can also zoom in or out
with the Microsoft IntelliMouse
by holding down the Ctrl key
as you move the wheel.

START WORD

When you start Word, a blank document appears. You can type text into this document.

START WORD

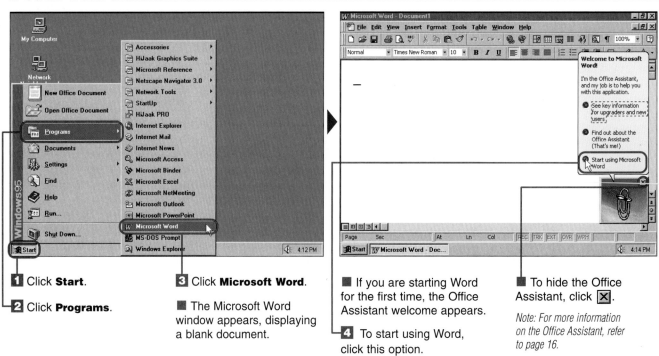

1 Click **Start**.

2 Click **Programs**.

3 Click **Microsoft Word**.

■ The Microsoft Word window appears, displaying a blank document.

■ If you are starting Word for the first time, the Office Assistant welcome appears.

4 To start using Word, click this option.

■ To hide the Office Assistant, click ⊠.

Note: For more information on the Office Assistant, refer to page 16.

The Word screen displays several items to help you perform tasks efficiently.

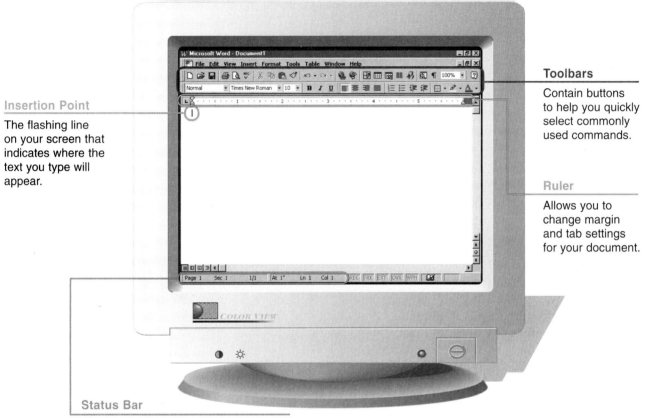

Insertion Point

The flashing line on your screen that indicates where the text you type will appear.

Toolbars

Contain buttons to help you quickly select commonly used commands.

Ruler

Allows you to change margin and tab settings for your document.

Status Bar

Displays information about the area of the document displayed on your screen and the position of the insertion point.

Page 1

The page displayed on your screen.

Sec 1

The section of the document displayed on your screen.

1/1

The page displayed on the screen and the total number of pages in the document.

At 1"

The distance from the top of the page to the insertion point.

Ln 1

The number of lines from the top of the page to the insertion point.

Col 1

The number of characters from the left margin to the insertion point, including spaces.

LENTER TEXT

Word lets you type text into your document quickly and easily.

I like to type.

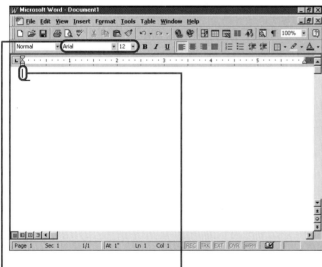

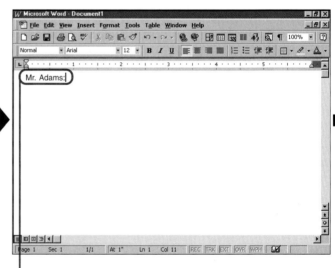

■ In this book, the design and size of text were changed to make the document easier to read. To change the design and size of text, refer to pages 94 and 95.

■ The flashing line on your screen, called the **insertion point**, indicates where the text you type will appear.

1 Type the first line of text.

2 To start a new paragraph, press the **Enter** key twice.

Can I enter symbols that are not available on my keyboard?

If you type one of the following sets of characters, Word will instantly replace the characters with a symbol. This lets you quickly enter symbols that are not available on your keyboard. To add other symbols to your document, refer to page 106.

(c)	©
(r)	®
(tm)	TM
:(	☹
:)	☺
:|	☺
<--	←
-->	→
<==	⬅
==>	➡
<=>	⬌

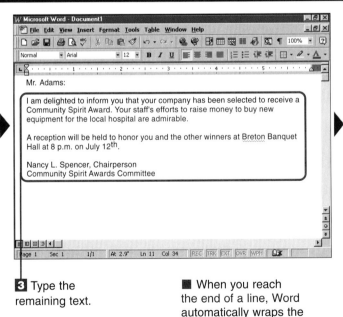

3 Type the remaining text.

■ When you reach the end of a line, Word automatically wraps the text to the next line. You only need to press **Enter** when you want to start a new line or paragraph.

■ Word automatically underlines misspelled words in red and grammar mistakes in green. The red and green underlines will not appear when you print your document.

Note: To correct spelling and grammar errors, refer to page 70.

SELECT TEXT

Before performing many tasks in Word, you must select the text you want to work with. Selected text appears highlighted on your screen.

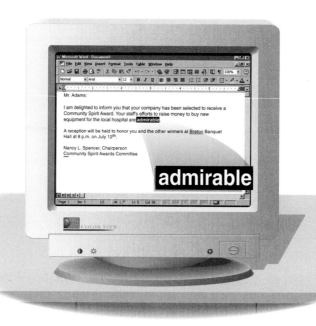

admirable

■ SELECT TEXT ■

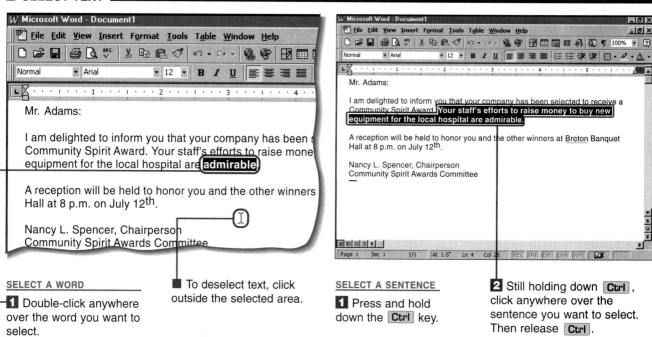

SELECT A WORD

1 Double-click anywhere over the word you want to select.

■ To deselect text, click outside the selected area.

SELECT A SENTENCE

1 Press and hold down the **Ctrl** key.

2 Still holding down **Ctrl**, click anywhere over the sentence you want to select. Then release **Ctrl**.

How do I select all the text in my document?

To quickly select all the text in your document, press and hold down the `Ctrl` key and then press the `A` key. Then release both keys.

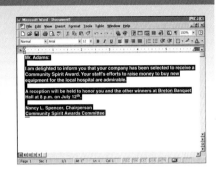

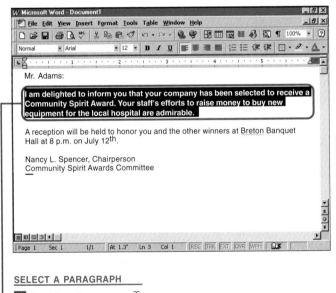

SELECT A PARAGRAPH

1 Position the mouse I anywhere over the paragraph you want to select and then quickly click **three** times.

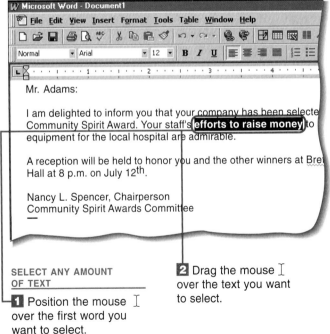

SELECT ANY AMOUNT OF TEXT

1 Position the mouse I over the first word you want to select.

2 Drag the mouse I over the text you want to select.

MOVE THROUGH A DOCUMENT

You can easily move to another location in your document.

If you create a long document, your computer screen cannot display all the text at the same time. You must scroll up or down to view and edit other parts of the document.

■ MOVE THE INSERTION POINT

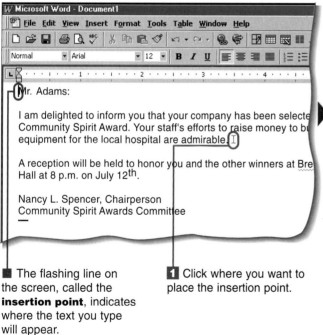

■ The flashing line on the screen, called the **insertion point**, indicates where the text you type will appear.

1 Click where you want to place the insertion point.

■ The insertion point appears in the new location.

Note: You can also press the ↑, ↓, ← or → keys to move the insertion point one line or character in any direction.

■ You cannot move the insertion point below the horizontal line displayed on the screen. To move this line, position the insertion point after the last character in the document and then press **Enter** several times.

?

How do I use the new Microsoft IntelliMouse to scroll?

The Microsoft IntelliMouse has a wheel between the left and right mouse buttons. Moving this wheel lets you quickly scroll through a document.

■ SCROLL UP OR DOWN

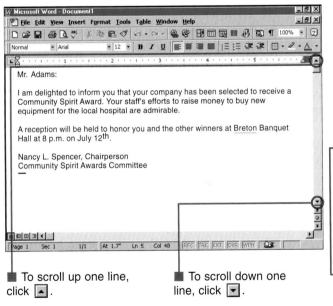

■ To scroll up one line, click ▲.

■ To scroll down one line, click ▼.

■ SCROLL TO ANY POSITION

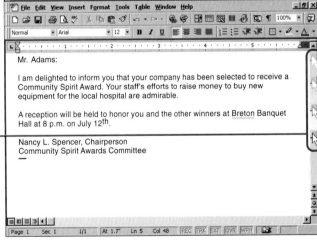

1 To quickly scroll through the document, drag the scroll box (▨) up or down the scroll bar.

■ The location of the scroll box indicates which part of the document you are viewing. To view the middle of the document, drag the scroll box halfway down the scroll bar.

GETTING HELP

If you do not know how to perform a task, you can ask the Office Assistant for help.

■ GETTING HELP (Using Office Assistant) ■

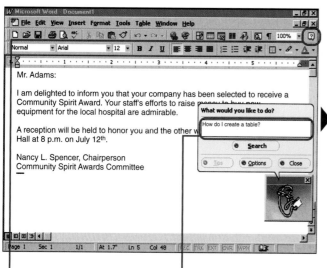

1 To display the Office Assistant, click 🔲.

2 Type the question you want to ask and then press the **Enter** key.

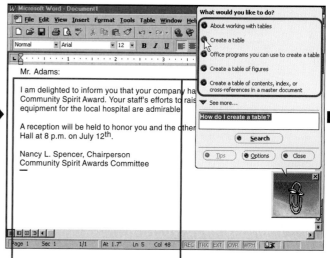

■ The Office Assistant displays a list of help topics that relate to the question you asked.

Note: If you do not see a help topic of interest, try rephrasing your question. Type the new question and then press the **Enter** *key.*

3 Click the help topic you want information on.

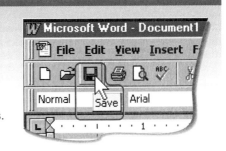

How do I display the name of a toolbar button?

To display the name of a toolbar button, position the mouse over the button. After a few seconds, the name of the button appears.

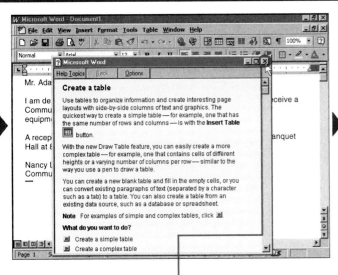

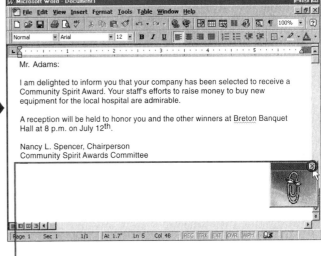

■ The Help window appears, displaying information about the topic you selected.

4 When you finish reading the information, click ☒ to close the Help window.

5 To hide the Office Assistant, click ☒.

GETTING HELP

You can use Word's extensive
help index to find information
the same way you would use
the index of a book.

■ GETTING HELP (Using Index)

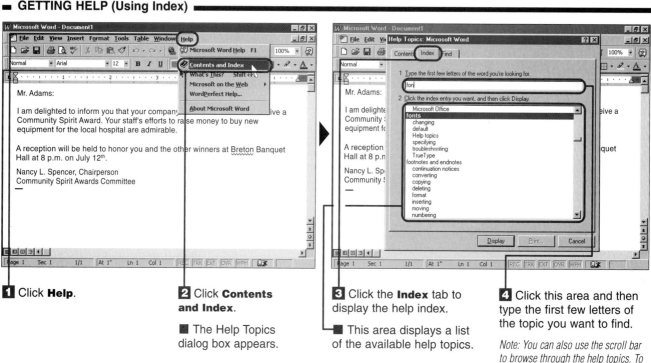

1 Click **Help**.

2 Click **Contents and Index**.

■ The Help Topics dialog box appears.

3 Click the **Index** tab to display the help index.

■ This area displays a list of the available help topics.

4 Click this area and then type the first few letters of the topic you want to find.

Note: You can also use the scroll bar to browse through the help topics. To use the scroll bar, refer to page 15.

Are there other ways to get help in Word?

There are three ways to get help in the Help Topics dialog box.

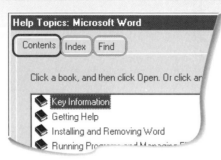

• Click the **Index** tab to view an alphabetical list of all the help topics.

• Click the **Find** tab to view all the help topics that contain a word or phrase of interest.

Note: You can also use the Office Assistant to get help. For information on the Office Assistant, refer to page 16.

• Click the **Contents** tab to browse through the help topics by subject.

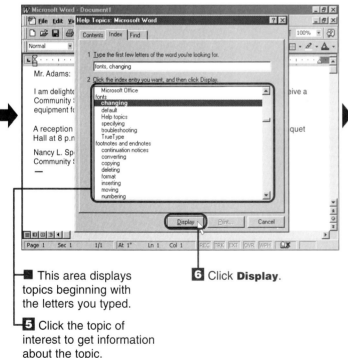

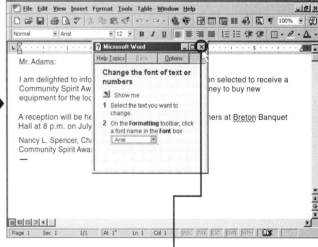

■ This area displays topics beginning with the letters you typed.

5 Click the topic of interest to get information about the topic.

6 Click **Display**.

■ A window appears, displaying information about the topic you selected.

7 When you finish reviewing the information, click ☒ to close the window.

CHAPTER 2

Save and Open Your Documents

How do I save and open my documents? How can I find a document if I do not remember its name? Learn how to manage your Word documents in this chapter.

SAVE A DOCUMENT

You should save your document to store it for future use. This lets you later retrieve the document for reviewing or editing.

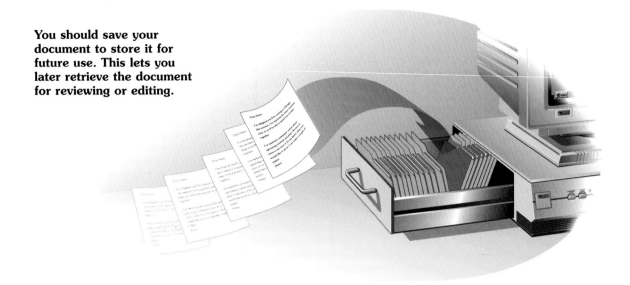

■ SAVE A DOCUMENT ■

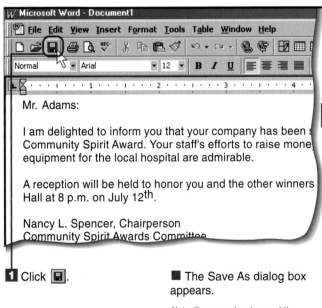

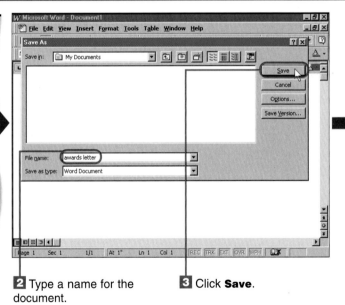

1 Click 🖫.

■ The Save As dialog box appears.

Note: If you previously saved the document, the Save As dialog box will not appear since you have already named the document.

2 Type a name for the document.

Note: You can use up to 255 characters to name a document.

3 Click **Save**.

Before you make major changes to a
document, save the document with
a different name. This gives you two
copies of the document—the original
document and a document with all
the changes.

SAVE A DOCUMENT WITH A NEW NAME

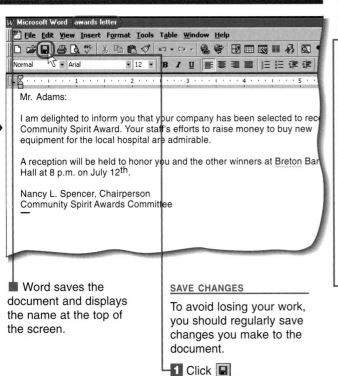

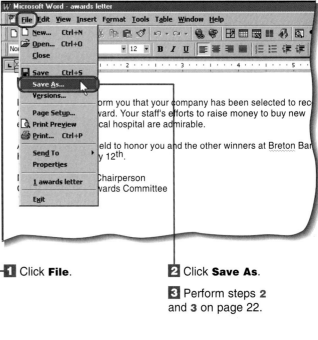

■ Word saves the
document and displays
the name at the top of
the screen.

SAVE CHANGES

To avoid losing your work,
you should regularly save
changes you make to the
document.

1 Click 🔲.

1 Click **File**.

2 Click **Save As**.

3 Perform steps **2**
and **3** on page 22.

SAVE A DOCUMENT IN A DIFFERENT FORMAT

You can save a Word document in a different format. This is useful if you need to share a document with a colleague who does not use Word 97.

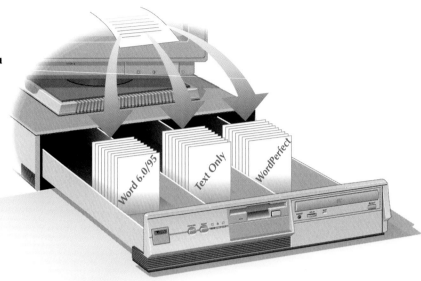

SAVE A DOCUMENT IN A DIFFERENT FORMAT

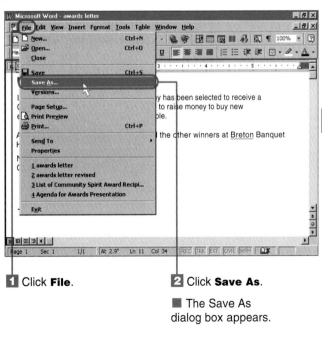

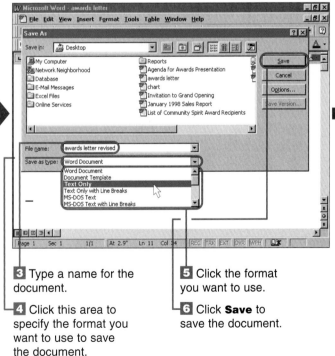

1 Click **File**.

2 Click **Save As**.

■ The Save As dialog box appears.

3 Type a name for the document.

4 Click this area to specify the format you want to use to save the document.

5 Click the format you want to use.

6 Click **Save** to save the document.

Which formats can I use to save my documents?

Word offers several formats that you can use to save your documents, including WordPerfect and previous versions of Word. If you are not sure which format to use, select the Text Only format. Most programs are capable of reading documents saved in the Text Only format.

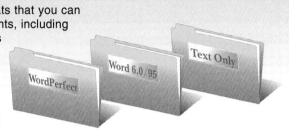

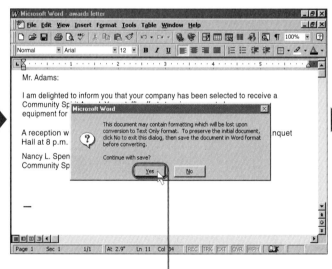

■ A dialog box may appear, indicating that some of the formatting in the document may be lost.

7 Click **Yes** to continue.

■ Word saves the document and displays the name at the top of the screen. You can now open and work with the document in another program.

PASSWORD PROTECT A DOCUMENT

You can prevent other people from reading and making changes to your document by protecting it with a password.

Passwords are case sensitive. For example, if your password is **Car**, you cannot type **car** or **CAR** to open the document.

■ PASSWORD PROTECT A DOCUMENT ■

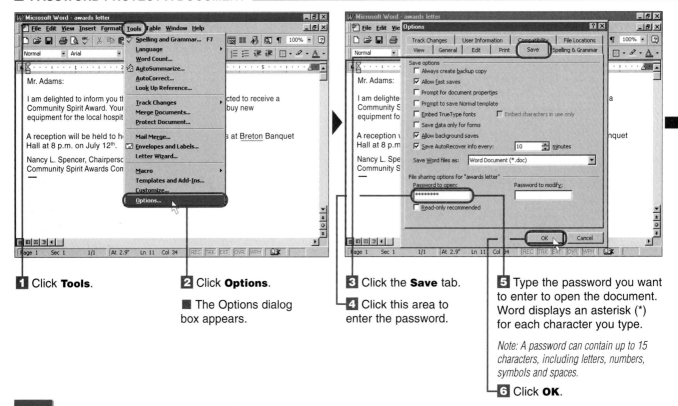

1 Click **Tools**.

2 Click **Options**.

■ The Options dialog box appears.

3 Click the **Save** tab.

4 Click this area to enter the password.

5 Type the password you want to enter to open the document. Word displays an asterisk (*) for each character you type.

Note: A password can contain up to 15 characters, including letters, numbers, symbols and spaces.

6 Click **OK**.

What happens if I forget the password I assigned to a document?

If you forget the password, you will not be able to open the document. Make sure you write down your password and store it in a safe place.

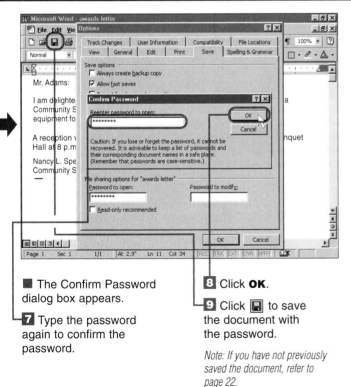

■ The Confirm Password dialog box appears.

7 Type the password again to confirm the password.

8 Click **OK**.

9 Click 🖫 to save the document with the password.

Note: If you have not previously saved the document, refer to page 22.

OPEN A PASSWORD-PROTECTED DOCUMENT

■ The Password dialog box appears when you try to open a password-protected document. To open a document, refer to page 30.

1 Type the password.

2 Click **OK**.

CLOSE A DOCUMENT

When you finish working with a document, you can close the document to remove it from your screen.

When you close a document, you do not exit the Word program. You can continue to work on other Word documents.

■ CLOSE A DOCUMENT

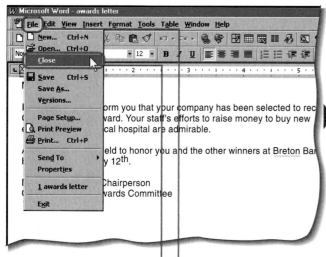

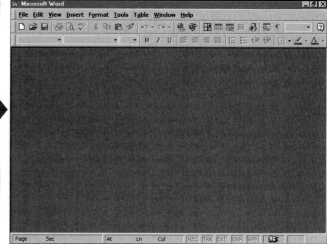

■ To save the document displayed on your screen before closing, refer to page 22.

1 To close the document, click **File**.

2 Click **Close**.

■ Word removes the document from your screen.

■ If you had more than one document open, the second last document you worked on would appear on the screen.

When you finish
using Word, you can
exit the program.

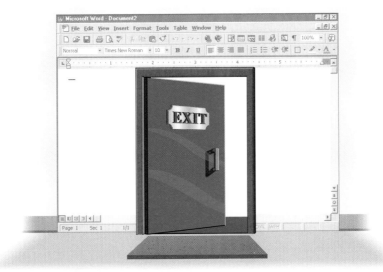

You should always
exit all programs
before turning off
your computer.

■ EXIT WORD

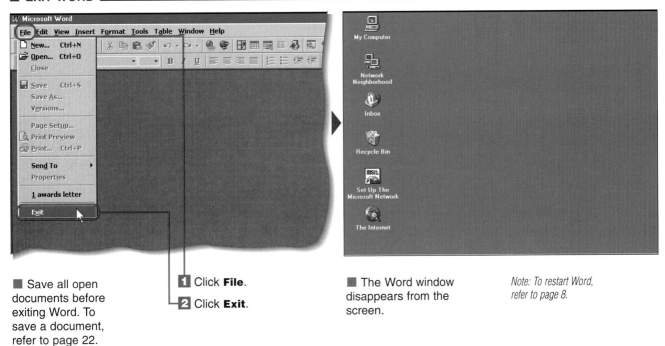

■ Save all open
documents before
exiting Word. To
save a document,
refer to page 22.

1 Click **File**.

2 Click **Exit**.

■ The Word window
disappears from the
screen.

*Note: To restart Word,
refer to page 8.*

OPEN A DOCUMENT

You can open a saved
document and display
it on your screen. This
allows you to review
and make changes to
your document.

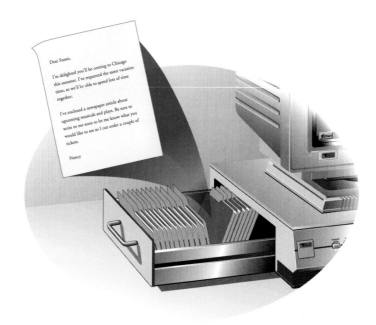

■ OPEN A DOCUMENT ■

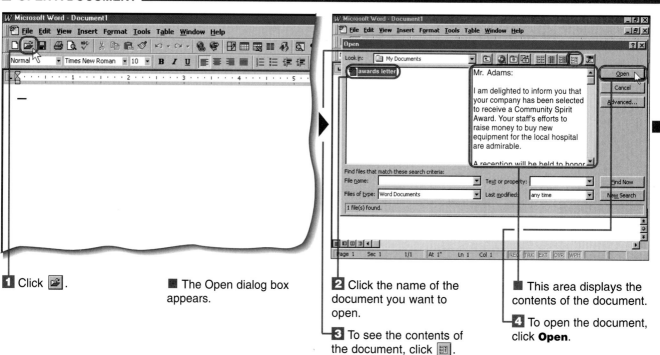

1 Click 📂.

■ The Open dialog box
appears.

2 Click the name of the
document you want to
open.

3 To see the contents of
the document, click 🔲.

■ This area displays the
contents of the document.

4 To open the document,
click **Open**.

Word remembers the names of the
last four documents you worked
with. You can quickly open any of
these documents.

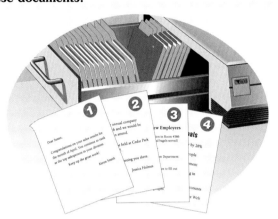

QUICKLY OPEN A DOCUMENT

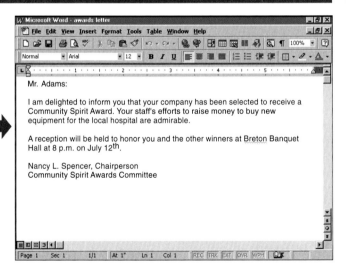

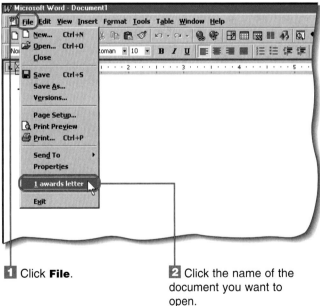

■ Word opens the
document and displays
it on the screen. You
can now review and
make changes to the
document.

1 Click **File**.

2 Click the name of the
document you want to
open.

OPEN A DOCUMENT IN A DIFFERENT FORMAT

You can use Word to open
and work with a document
that was created in another
program. This helps you
work with colleagues
who use different word
processing programs.

■ OPEN A DOCUMENT IN A DIFFERENT FORMAT ■

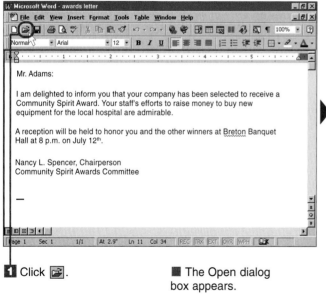

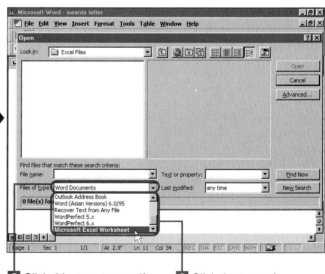

1 Click 📂.

■ The Open dialog
box appears.

2 Click this area to specify
the type of document you
want to open.

3 Click the type of
document you want
to open.

*Note: If you do not know the
type of document you want
to open, click* **All Files***.*

What types of documents can Word open?

Word can open documents created in many different programs, such as WordPerfect, Excel and older versions of Word for Windows and DOS. Word can also open HTML and Text Only documents.

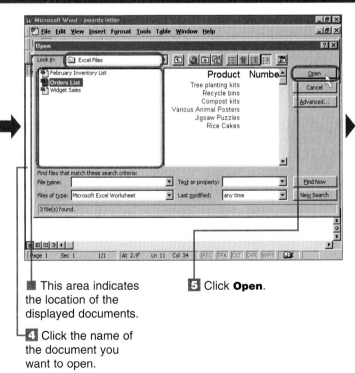

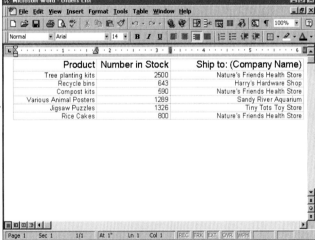

■ This area indicates the location of the displayed documents.

4 Click the name of the document you want to open.

5 Click **Open**.

■ Word opens the document and displays it on your screen. You can now review and make changes to the document.

FIND A DOCUMENT

If you cannot remember the name or location of a document you want to open, you can have Word search for the document.

■ FIND A DOCUMENT

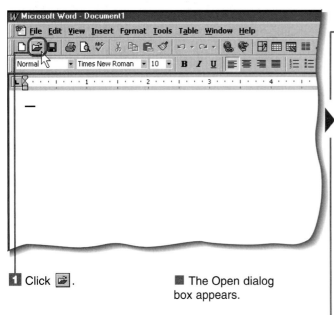

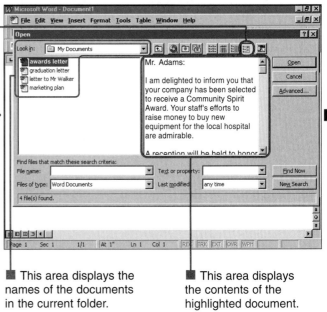

1 Click 📂.

■ The Open dialog box appears.

■ This area displays the names of the documents in the current folder.

2 To see the contents of the highlighted document, click 🖾.

■ This area displays the contents of the highlighted document.

Note: To display the contents of another document, click the name of the document.

Can Word find a document if I know only part of the document name?

Word will find all the documents with names that contain the text you specify. For example, searching for **letter** will find **letter to Susan**, **graduation letter** and **my letter**.

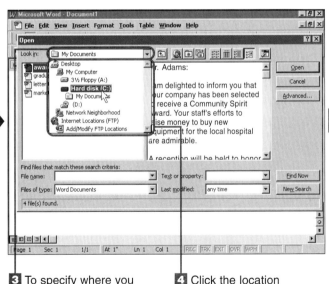

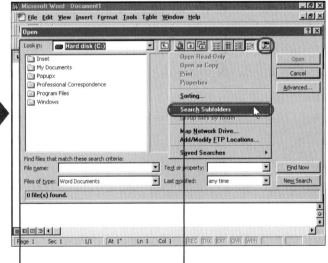

3 To specify where you want Word to search for the document, click this area.

4 Click the location you want to search.

5 To search the contents of all the folders in the location you selected, click [image].

6 Click **Search Subfolders**.

CONTINUED

FIND A DOCUMENT

When the search is complete, Word displays the names of the documents it found.

Documents Found
1) 1996 Awards
2) 1997 Awards
3) Awards Ceremony
4) Award Descriptions
5) Award Nominees

■ **FIND A DOCUMENT** (CONTINUED) ■

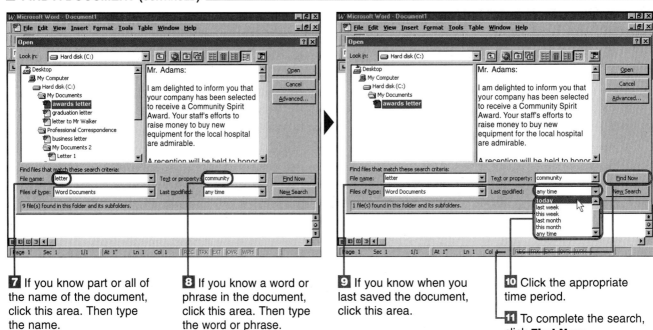

7 If you know part or all of the name of the document, click this area. Then type the name.

8 If you know a word or phrase in the document, click this area. Then type the word or phrase.

9 If you know when you last saved the document, click this area.

10 Click the appropriate time period.

11 To complete the search, click **Find Now**.

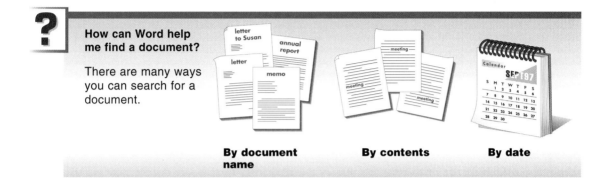

? **How can Word help me find a document?**

There are many ways you can search for a document.

By document name **By contents** **By date**

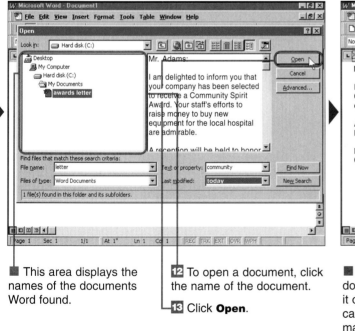

■ This area displays the names of the documents Word found.

12 To open a document, click the name of the document.

13 Click **Open**.

■ Word opens the document and displays it on your screen. You can now review and make changes to the document.

CHAPTER 3

Change Document Display

Can I change the appearance of my Word screen? This chapter will teach you how to customize your screen to suit your needs.

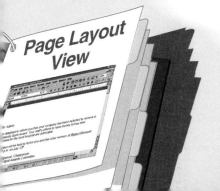

Page Layout View

CHANGE THE VIEW

Word offers four different ways to display your document. You can choose the view that best suits your needs.

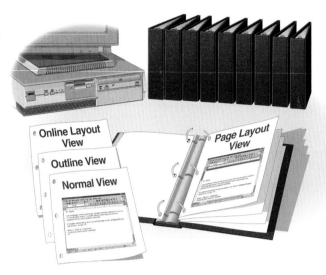

- Online Layout View
- Outline View
- Normal View
- Page Layout View

CHANGE THE VIEW

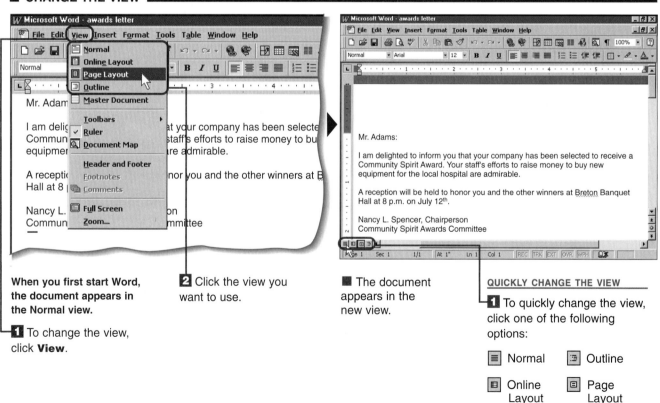

When you first start Word, the document appears in the Normal view.

1 To change the view, click **View**.

2 Click the view you want to use.

■ The document appears in the new view.

QUICKLY CHANGE THE VIEW

1 To quickly change the view, click one of the following options:

☰ Normal	⊞ Outline
▣ Online Layout	▤ Page Layout

THE FOUR VIEWS

Normal View

This view simplifies the document so you can quickly enter, edit and format text. The Normal view does not display top or bottom margins, headers, footers or page numbers.

Outline View

This view helps you review and work with the structure of a document. You can focus on the main headings by hiding the remaining text.

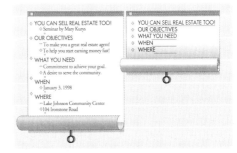

Page Layout View

This view displays the document as it will appear on a printed page. The Page Layout view displays top and bottom margins, headers, footers and page numbers.

Online Layout View

This view displays documents so they are easy to read on the screen. The Online Layout view displays a document map, which lets you move quickly to specific locations in your document.

ZOOM IN OR OUT

Word lets you enlarge or reduce the display of text on your screen.

Changing the zoom setting will not affect the way the document appears on a printed page.

ZOOM IN OR OUT

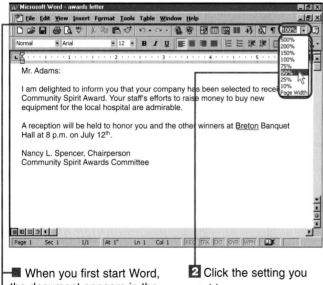

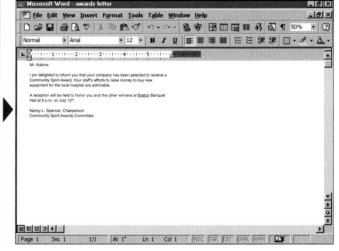

■ When you first start Word, the document appears in the 100% zoom setting.

1 To display a list of zoom settings, click ▾ in this area.

2 Click the setting you want to use.

■ The document appears in the new zoom setting. You can edit your document as usual.

■ To return to the normal zoom setting, repeat steps **1** and **2**, selecting **100%** in step **2**.

You can use the ruler to position text on a page. You can display or hide the ruler at any time.

When you first start Word, the ruler is displayed on your screen. Hiding the ruler provides a larger and less cluttered working area.

■ DISPLAY OR HIDE THE RULER

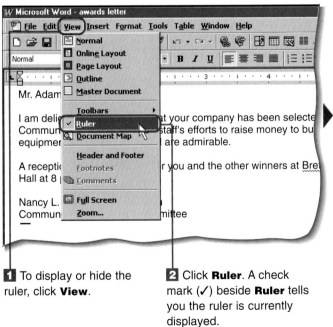

1 To display or hide the ruler, click **View**.

2 Click **Ruler**. A check mark (✓) beside **Ruler** tells you the ruler is currently displayed.

■ Word displays or hides the ruler.

DISPLAY OR HIDE TOOLBARS

Word offers several toolbars that you can hide or display at any time. Each toolbar contains buttons that help you quickly perform common tasks.

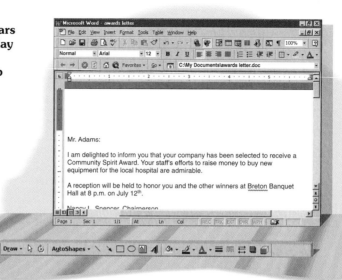

■ DISPLAY OR HIDE TOOLBARS ■

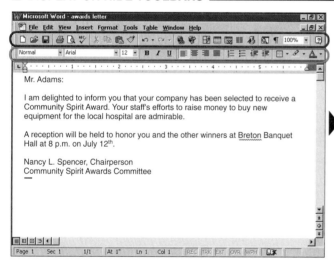

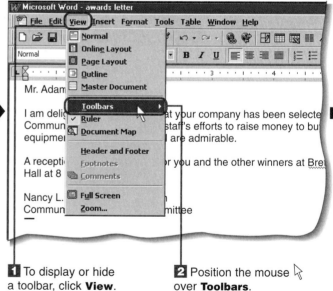

When you first start Word, the Standard and Formatting toolbars appear on the screen.

Standard toolbar

Formatting toolbar

1 To display or hide a toolbar, click **View**.

2 Position the mouse ⤺ over **Toolbars**.

Why would I want to hide a toolbar?

A screen displaying fewer toolbars provides a larger and less cluttered working area.

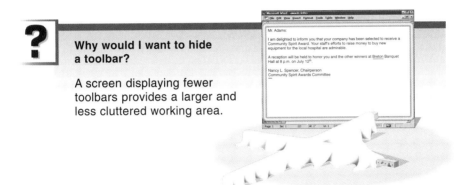

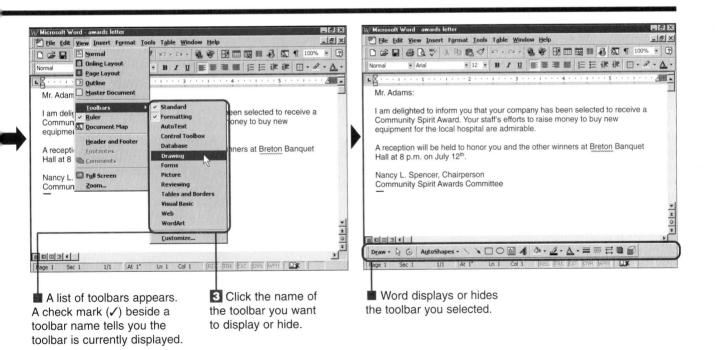

■ A list of toolbars appears. A check mark (✓) beside a toolbar name tells you the toolbar is currently displayed.

3 Click the name of the toolbar you want to display or hide.

■ Word displays or hides the toolbar you selected.

USING THE DOCUMENT MAP

You can use the Document Map to move through a document.

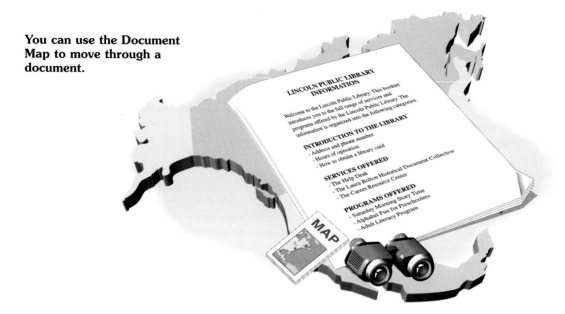

■ **USING THE DOCUMENT MAP**

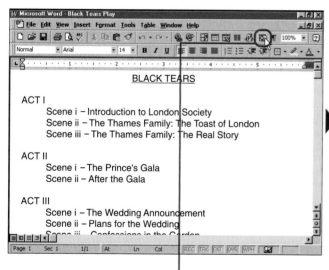

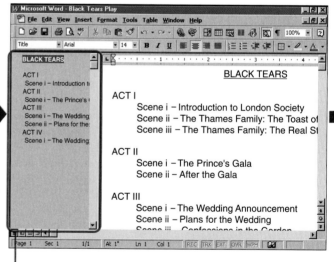

■ For this example, a new document was created.

1 To display the Document Map, click 🔲.

■ The Document Map appears and shows the main headings in your document.

Note: If Word does not find any headings in your document, the Document Map is blank.

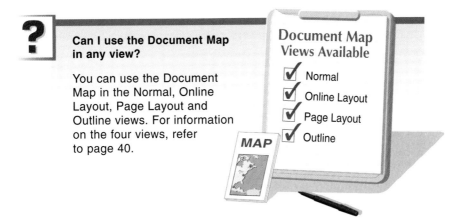

Can I use the Document Map in any view?

You can use the Document Map in the Normal, Online Layout, Page Layout and Outline views. For information on the four views, refer to page 40.

Document Map Views Available

☑ Normal
☑ Online Layout
☑ Page Layout
☑ Outline

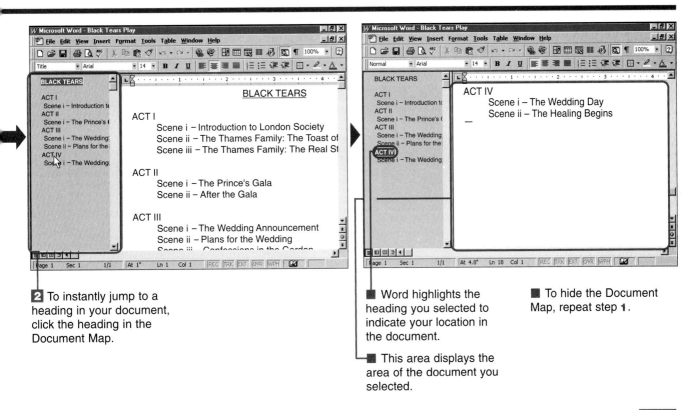

2 To instantly jump to a heading in your document, click the heading in the Document Map.

■ Word highlights the heading you selected to indicate your location in the document.

■ This area displays the area of the document you selected.

■ To hide the Document Map, repeat step **1**.

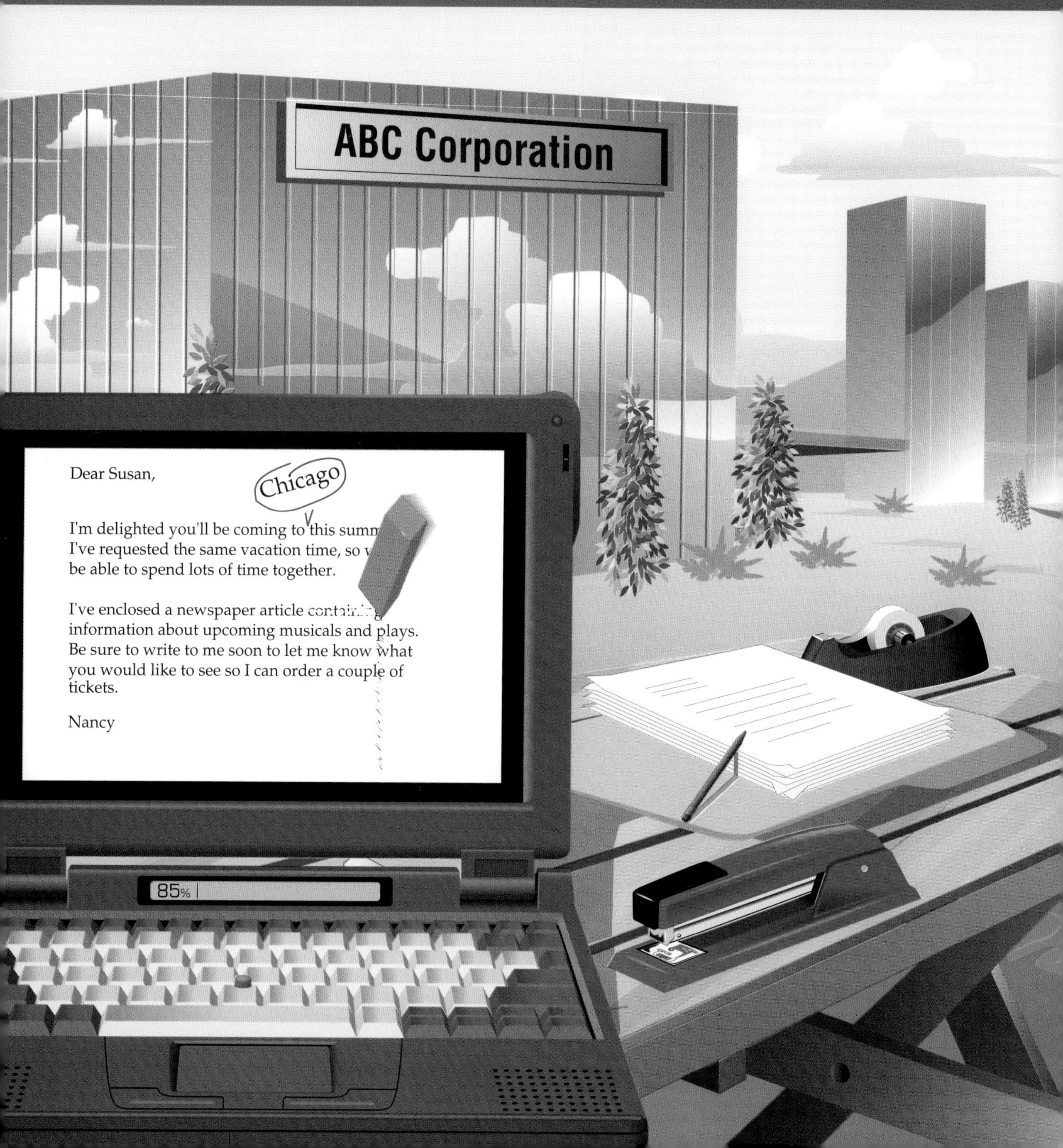

ABC Corporation

Dear Susan,

Chicago

I'm delighted you'll be coming to this summ
I've requested the same vacation time, so w
be able to spend lots of time together.

I've enclosed a newspaper article containing
information about upcoming musicals and plays.
Be sure to write to me soon to let me know what
you would like to see so I can order a couple of
tickets.

Nancy

85%

CHAPTER 4

Edit Your Documents

Wondering how to edit the text in your documents quickly and efficiently? Learn many time-saving techniques, including moving and copying text, and much more.

INSERT TEXT

You can easily add new text to your document. The existing text will move to make room for the text you add.

INSERT CHARACTERS

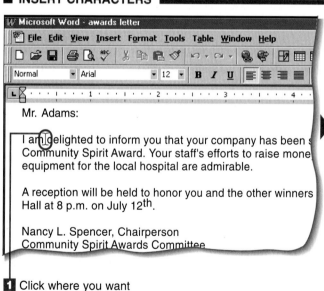

1 Click where you want to insert the new text.

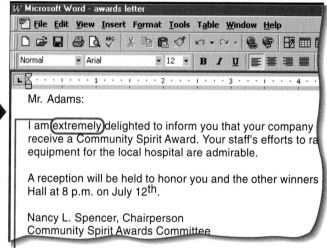

2 Type the text you want to insert. To insert a blank space, press the **Spacebar**.

■ The words to the right of the new text move forward.

How do I insert symbols into my document?

Word will automatically replace specific characters you type with symbols. This lets you quickly enter symbols that are not available on your keyboard.

Note: For more information on inserting symbols, refer to page 106.

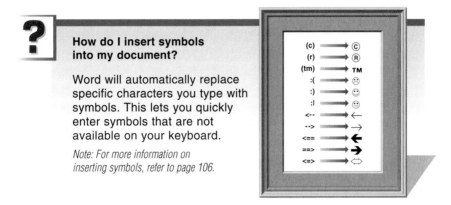

■ INSERT A BLANK LINE

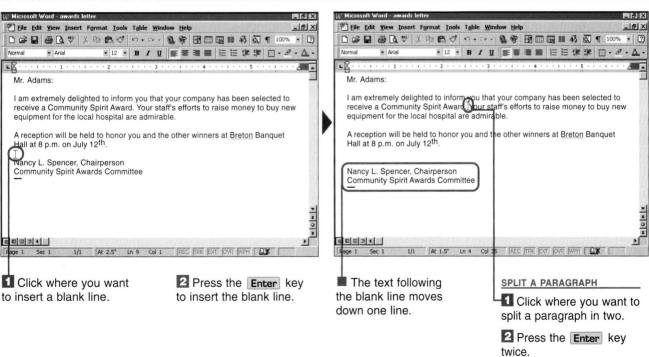

1 Click where you want to insert a blank line.

2 Press the `Enter` key to insert the blank line.

■ The text following the blank line moves down one line.

SPLIT A PARAGRAPH

1 Click where you want to split a paragraph in two.

2 Press the `Enter` key twice.

DELETE TEXT

You can easily remove text you no longer need. The remaining text moves to fill any empty spaces.

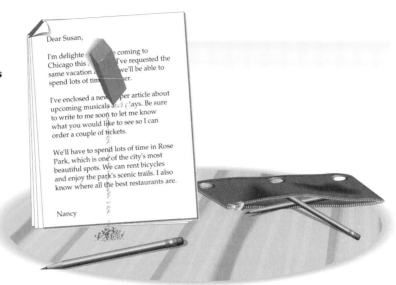

DELETE CHARACTERS

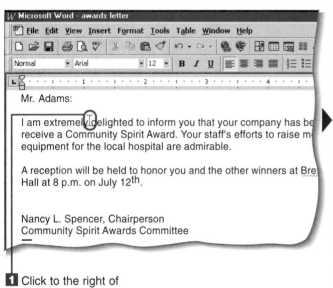

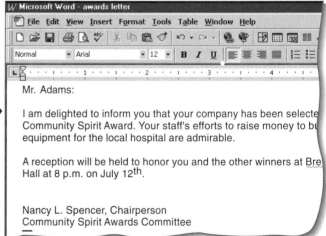

1 Click to the right of the first character you want to delete.

2 Press the ◆Backspace key once for each character or space you want to delete.

■ You can also use the Delete key to remove characters. Click to the left of the first character you want to remove. Press the Delete key once for each character or space you want to remove.

Can I recover text I accidentally delete?

Word remembers the last changes you made to your document. If you regret deleting text, you can use the Undo feature to undo the change.

Note: For information on the Undo feature, refer to page 55.

> Dear Susan,
>
> I'm delighted you'll be coming to Chicago *this* summer. I've requested the same vacation time, so we'll be able to spend lots of time together.

DELETE A BLANK LINE

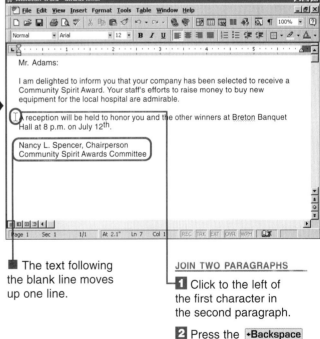

1 Click the beginning of the blank line you want to delete.

2 Press the ◆Backspace key to remove the blank line.

■ The text following the blank line moves up one line.

JOIN TWO PARAGRAPHS

1 Click to the left of the first character in the second paragraph.

2 Press the ◆Backspace key until the paragraphs are joined.

DELETE TEXT

You can quickly
delete text you
have selected.

DELETE SELECTED TEXT

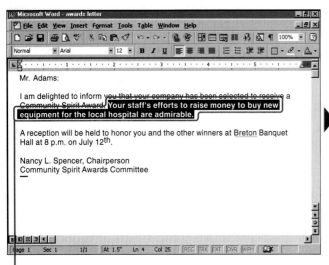

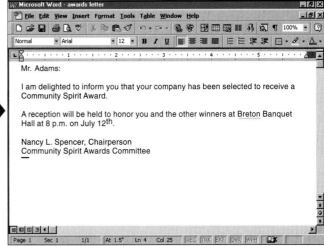

1 Select the text you
want to delete. To select
text, refer to page 12.

2 Press the Delete key
to remove the text.

UNDO LAST CHANGE

Word remembers the last changes you made to your document. If you regret these changes, you can cancel them by using the Undo feature.

UNDO LAST CHANGE

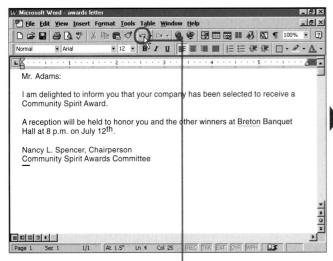

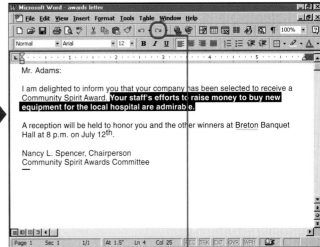

The Undo feature can cancel your last editing and formatting changes.

1 To undo your last change, click the undo icon.

■ Word cancels the last change you made to your document.

■ You can repeat step 1 to cancel previous changes you made.

■ To reverse the results of using the Undo feature, click the redo icon.

CHANGE CASE OF TEXT

You can change the case of text in your document without having to retype the text. Word offers five case options you can choose from.

■ CHANGE CASE OF TEXT

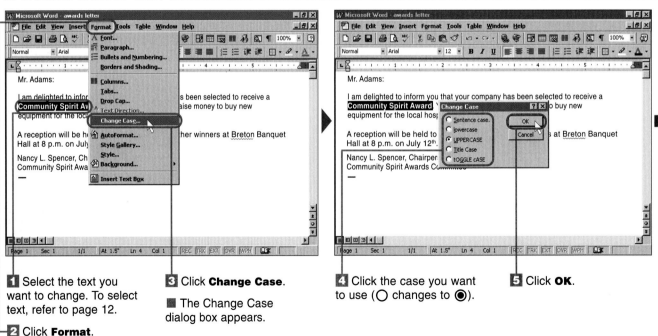

1 Select the text you want to change. To select text, refer to page 12.

2 Click **Format**.

3 Click **Change Case**.

■ The Change Case dialog box appears.

4 Click the case you want to use (○ changes to ◉).

5 Click **OK**.

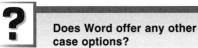

Does Word offer any other case options?

You can find more case options in the Font dialog box, such as Small caps and All caps. To change the appearance of text using the Font dialog box, refer to pages 98 to 101.

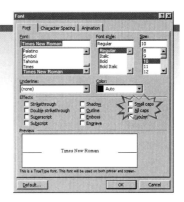

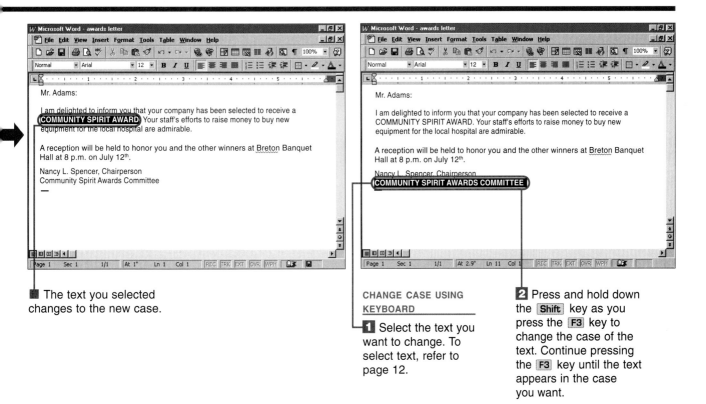

■ The text you selected changes to the new case.

CHANGE CASE USING KEYBOARD

1 Select the text you want to change. To select text, refer to page 12.

2 Press and hold down the **Shift** key as you press the **F3** key to change the case of the text. Continue pressing the **F3** key until the text appears in the case you want.

MOVE TEXT

You can reorganize your
document by moving
text from one location
to another.

■ MOVE TEXT ■

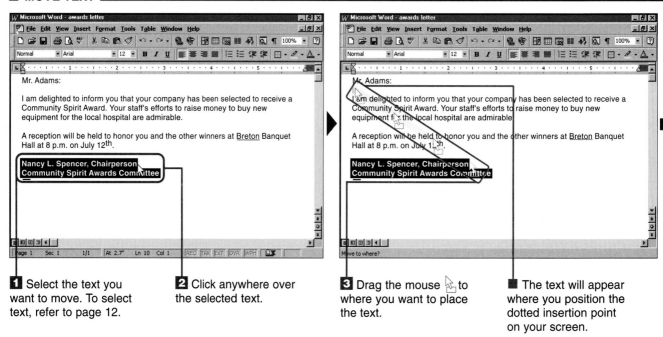

1 Select the text you
want to move. To select
text, refer to page 12.

2 Click anywhere over
the selected text.

3 Drag the mouse 📄 to
where you want to place
the text.

■ The text will appear
where you position the
dotted insertion point
on your screen.

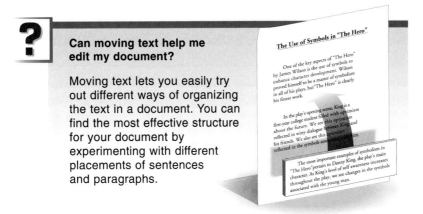

Can moving text help me edit my document?

Moving text lets you easily try out different ways of organizing the text in a document. You can find the most effective structure for your document by experimenting with different placements of sentences and paragraphs.

■ MOVE TEXT USING TOOLBAR BUTTONS ■

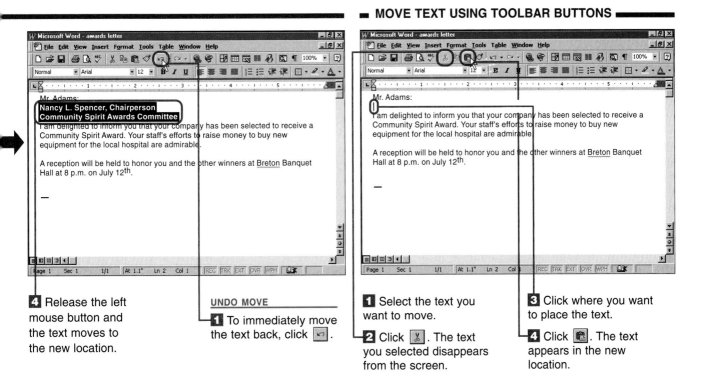

4 Release the left mouse button and the text moves to the new location.

UNDO MOVE

1 To immediately move the text back, click [↶].

1 Select the text you want to move.

2 Click [✂]. The text you selected disappears from the screen.

3 Click where you want to place the text.

4 Click [📋]. The text appears in the new location.

COPY TEXT

You can place a copy of text in a different location in your document. This will save you time since you do not have to retype the text.

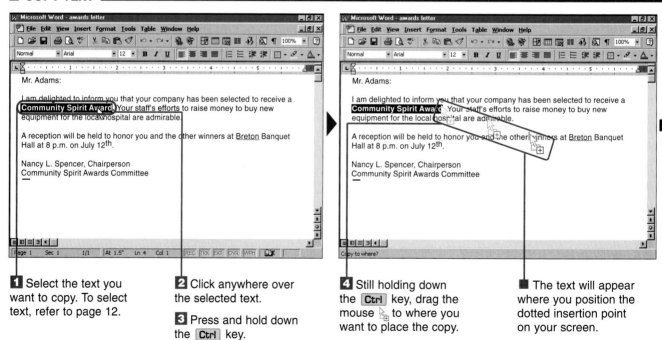

1 Select the text you want to copy. To select text, refer to page 12.

2 Click anywhere over the selected text.

3 Press and hold down the **Ctrl** key.

4 Still holding down the **Ctrl** key, drag the mouse to where you want to place the copy.

■ The text will appear where you position the dotted insertion point on your screen.

How can copying text help me edit my document?

If you plan to make major changes to a paragraph, you may want to copy the paragraph before you begin. This gives you two copies of the paragraph—the original paragraph and a paragraph with all the changes.

COPY TEXT USING TOOLBAR BUTTONS

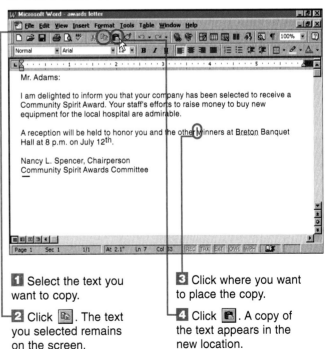

5 Release the left mouse button and then release the **Ctrl** key.

■ A copy of the text appears in the new location.

UNDO COPY

1 To immediately remove the copy, click 🔄.

1 Select the text you want to copy.

2 Click 📋. The text you selected remains on the screen.

3 Click where you want to place the copy.

4 Click 📋. A copy of the text appears in the new location.

FIND TEXT

You can use the Find feature to locate a word or phrase in your document.

■ FIND TEXT ■

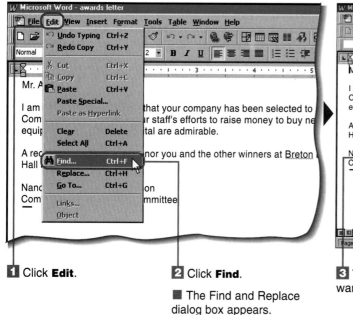

1 Click **Edit**.

2 Click **Find**.

■ The Find and Replace dialog box appears.

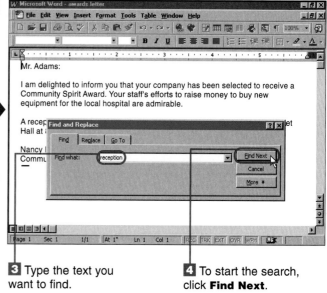

3 Type the text you want to find.

4 To start the search, click **Find Next**.

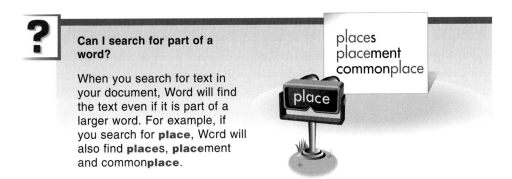

Can I search for part of a word?

When you search for text in your document, Word will find the text even if it is part of a larger word. For example, if you search for **place**, Word will also find **place**s, **place**ment and common**place**.

places
placement
commonplace

place

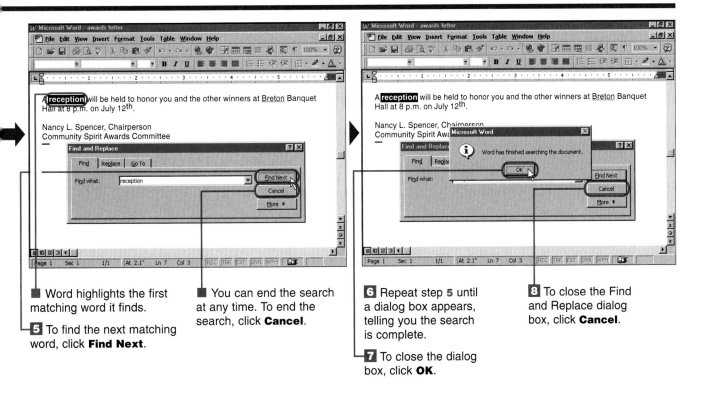

■ Word highlights the first matching word it finds.

5 To find the next matching word, click **Find Next**.

■ You can end the search at any time. To end the search, click **Cancel**.

6 Repeat step **5** until a dialog box appears, telling you the search is complete.

7 To close the dialog box, click **OK**.

8 To close the Find and Replace dialog box, click **Cancel**.

FIND TEXT

Word provides several advanced options to help you find the exact text you want.

Match case

Find words with exactly matching upper and lower case letters.

Find whole words only

Find a word only if it is not part of a larger word.

■ FIND TEXT (Advanced Options)

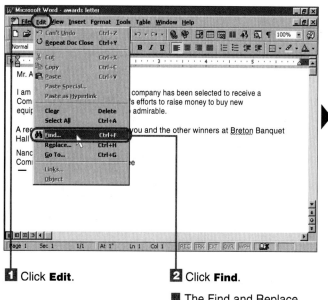

1 Click **Edit**.

2 Click **Find**.

■ The Find and Replace dialog box appears.

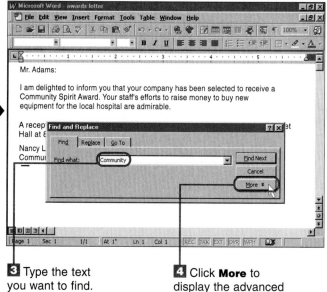

3 Type the text you want to find.

4 Click **More** to display the advanced searching options.

Use wildcards

Use wildcard characters to find text.

Note: The asterisk (*) wildcard represents many characters. The question mark (?) wildcard represents a single character.

Sounds like

Find words that sound the same but are spelled differently.

Find all word forms

Find all forms of the word you search for.

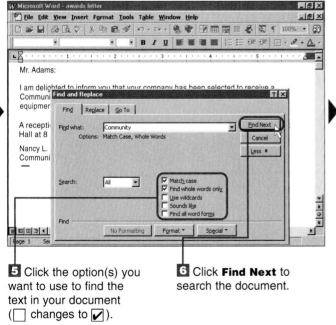

5 Click the option(s) you want to use to find the text in your document (☐ changes to ✔).

6 Click **Find Next** to search the document.

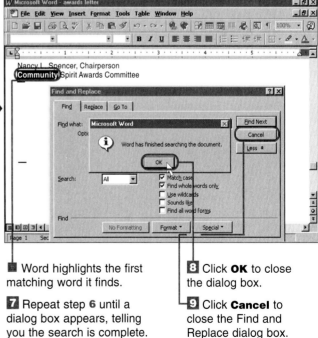

Word highlights the first matching word it finds.

7 Repeat step **6** until a dialog box appears, telling you the search is complete.

8 Click **OK** to close the dialog box.

9 Click **Cancel** to close the Find and Replace dialog box.

REPLACE TEXT

The Replace feature can
locate and replace every
occurrence of a word or
phrase in your document.
This is ideal if you have
frequently misspelled
a name.

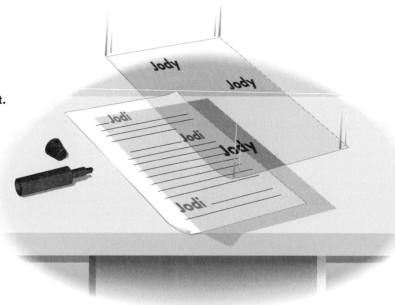

■ REPLACE TEXT

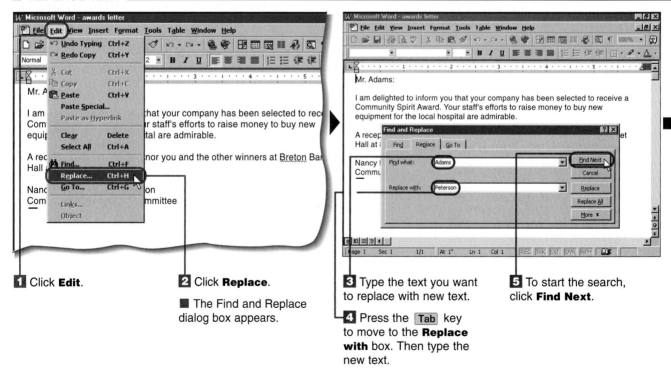

1 Click **Edit**.

2 Click **Replace**.

■ The Find and Replace
dialog box appears.

3 Type the text you want
to replace with new text.

4 Press the `Tab` key
to move to the **Replace
with** box. Then type the
new text.

5 To start the search,
click **Find Next**.

? Can I use the Replace feature to enter text more quickly?

The Replace feature is useful if you have to type a long word or phrase (example: University of Massachusetts) many times in a document.

You can type a short form of the word or phrase (example: UM) throughout your document and then have Word replace the short form with the full word or phrase.

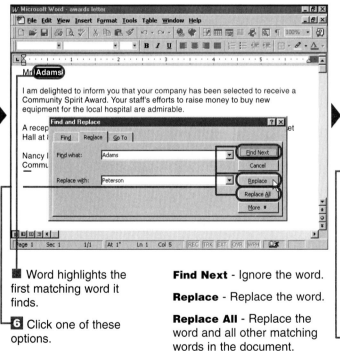

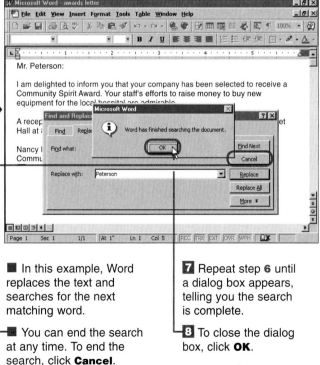

■ Word highlights the first matching word it finds.

6 Click one of these options.

Find Next - Ignore the word.

Replace - Replace the word.

Replace All - Replace the word and all other matching words in the document.

■ In this example, Word replaces the text and searches for the next matching word.

■ You can end the search at any time. To end the search, click **Cancel**.

7 Repeat step **6** until a dialog box appears, telling you the search is complete.

8 To close the dialog box, click **OK**.

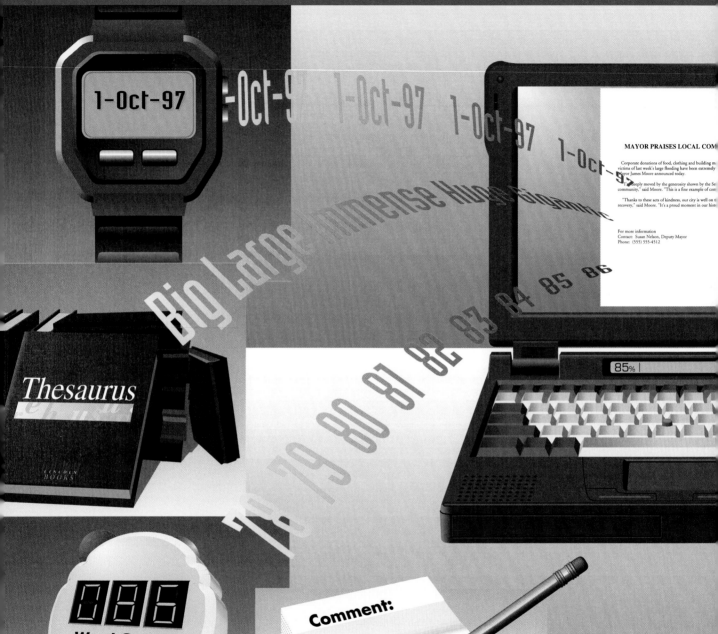

CHAPTER 5

Smart Editing

Do you want to check your documents for spelling and grammar errors? Would you like to insert the date and time or add comments? Find out how in this chapter.

CHECK SPELLING AND GRAMMAR

Word automatically checks your document for spelling and grammar errors as you type. You can easily correct these errors.

■ CORRECT AN ERROR ■

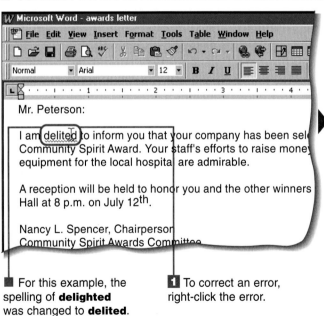

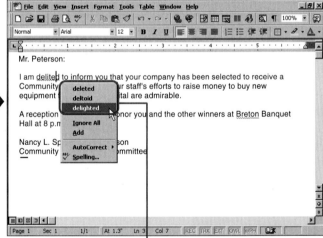

■ For this example, the spelling of **delighted** was changed to **delited**.

■ Word underlines misspelled words in red and grammar mistakes in green.

1 To correct an error, right-click the error.

■ A menu appears with suggestions to correct the error.

■ If Word does not display a suggestion you want to use, click outside the menu to hide the menu.

2 To select one of the suggestions, click the suggestion.

How will I know if my document contains an error?

Word underlines spelling errors in red and grammar errors in green. The underlines will not appear when you print your document.

Spelling Errors   **Grammar Errors**

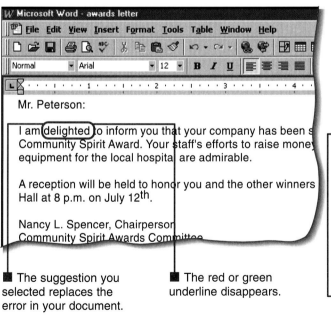

■ The suggestion you selected replaces the error in your document.

■ The red or green underline disappears.

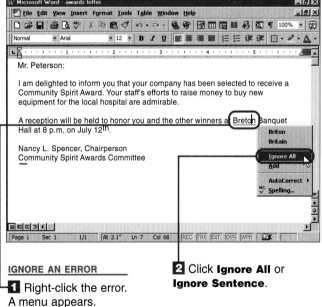

IGNORE AN ERROR

1 Right-click the error. A menu appears.

2 Click **Ignore All** or **Ignore Sentence**.

CHECK SPELLING AND GRAMMAR

When you finish typing your document, you can find and correct all spelling and grammar errors at once.

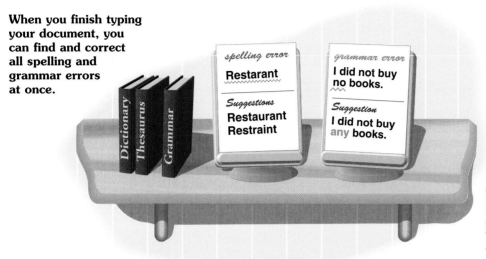

Word automatically underlines misspelled words in red and grammar mistakes in green. The red and green underlines will not appear when you print your document.

CORRECT ENTIRE DOCUMENT

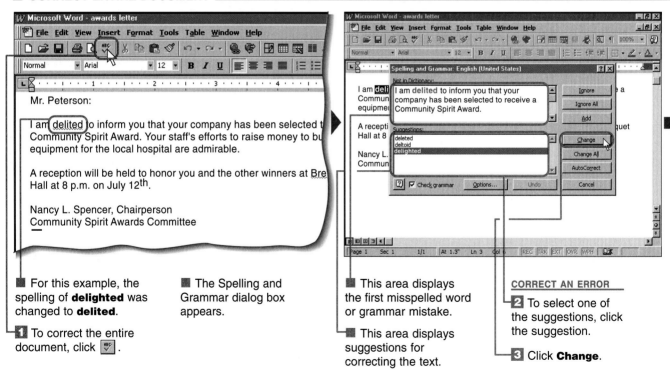

■ For this example, the spelling of **delighted** was changed to **delited**.

1 To correct the entire document, click 🔤.

■ The Spelling and Grammar dialog box appears.

■ This area displays the first misspelled word or grammar mistake.

■ This area displays suggestions for correcting the text.

CORRECT AN ERROR

2 To select one of the suggestions, click the suggestion.

3 Click **Change**.

Can Word automatically correct my typing mistakes?

Word automatically corrects common spelling errors as you type.

Note: For more information on using the AutoCorrect feature, refer to page 78.

adn ➡ and	
alot ➡ a lot	
comittee ➡ committee	
don;t ➡ don't	
nwe ➡ new	
occurence ➡ occurrence	
recieve ➡ receive	
seperate ➡ separate	
teh ➡ the	

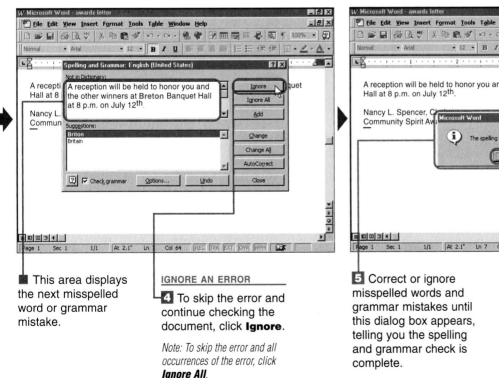

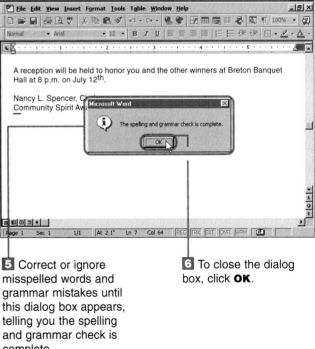

■ This area displays the next misspelled word or grammar mistake.

IGNORE AN ERROR

4 To skip the error and continue checking the document, click **Ignore**.

Note: To skip the error and all occurrences of the error, click ***Ignore All***.

5 Correct or ignore misspelled words and grammar mistakes until this dialog box appears, telling you the spelling and grammar check is complete.

6 To close the dialog box, click **OK**.

TURN OFF SPELLING AND GRAMMAR CHECK

You can turn off Word's automatic spelling and grammar check features. This is useful if you are distracted by the red and green underlines Word uses to indicate errors in your documents.

TURN OFF SPELLING AND GRAMMAR CHECK

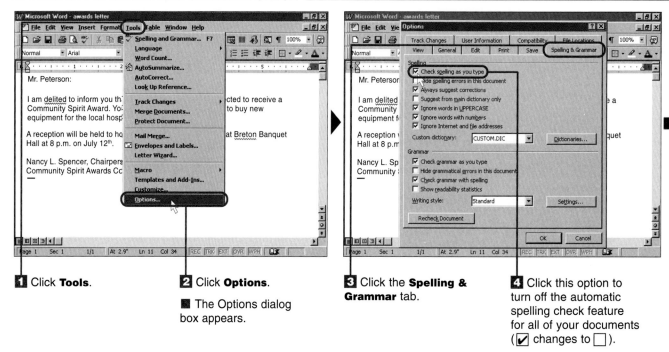

1 Click **Tools**.

2 Click **Options**.

■ The Options dialog box appears.

3 Click the **Spelling & Grammar** tab.

4 Click this option to turn off the automatic spelling check feature for all of your documents (☑ changes to ☐).

How can I find errors in my document after I turn off the automatic spelling and grammar check features?

You can check for spelling and grammar errors in your document at any time. For information, refer to page 72.

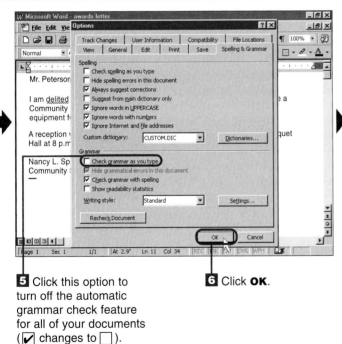

5 Click this option to turn off the automatic grammar check feature for all of your documents (☑ changes to ☐).

6 Click **OK**.

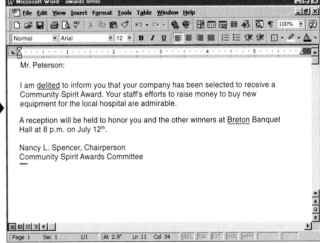

■ The misspelled words and grammar errors in the document are no longer underlined.

TURN ON SPELLING AND GRAMMAR CHECK

■ To turn on the automatic spelling and grammar check features at any time, repeat steps **1** to **6** (☐ changes to ☑ in steps **4** and **5**).

USING THE THESAURUS

You can use the Thesaurus to replace a word in your document with one that is more suitable.

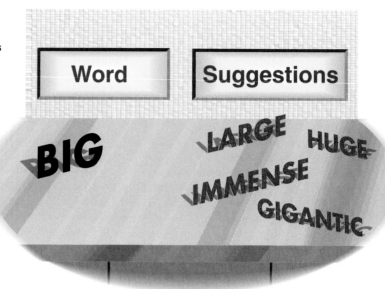

USING THE THESAURUS

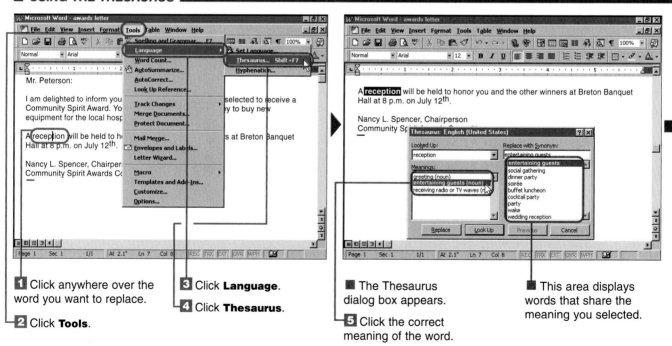

1 Click anywhere over the word you want to replace.

2 Click **Tools**.

3 Click **Language**.

4 Click **Thesaurus**.

■ The Thesaurus dialog box appears.

5 Click the correct meaning of the word.

■ This area displays words that share the meaning you selected.

How can the Thesaurus feature help me?

Using the Thesaurus included with Word is faster and more convenient than searching through a printed thesaurus.

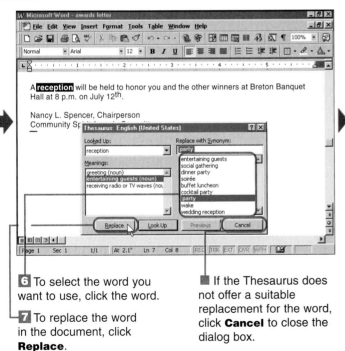

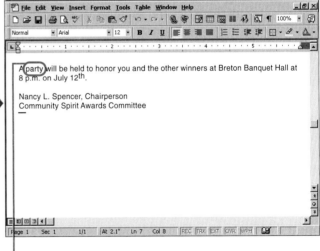

6 To select the word you want to use, click the word.

7 To replace the word in the document, click **Replace**.

■ If the Thesaurus does not offer a suitable replacement for the word, click **Cancel** to close the dialog box.

■ Your selection replaces the word in the document.

USING AUTOCORRECT

Word automatically corrects hundreds of common typing, spelling and grammar errors as you type. You can create an AutoCorrect entry to add your own words and phrases to the list.

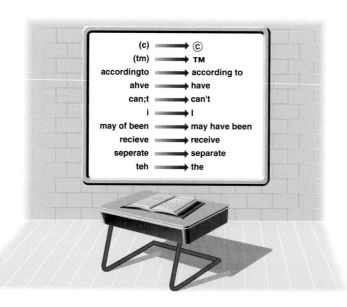

■ CREATE AN AUTOCORRECT ENTRY

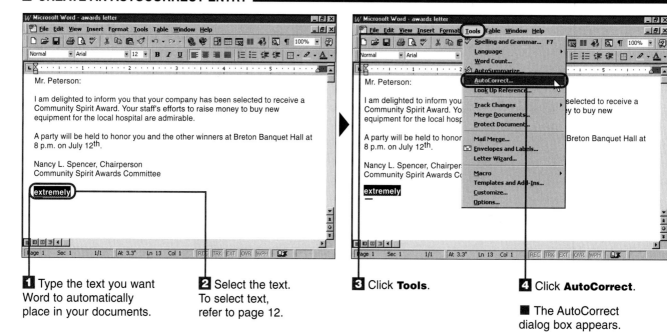

1 Type the text you want Word to automatically place in your documents.

2 Select the text. To select text, refer to page 12.

3 Click **Tools**.

4 Click **AutoCorrect**.

■ The AutoCorrect dialog box appears.

What types of AutoCorrect entries can I create?

You can create AutoCorrect entries for errors you commonly make and words and phrases you frequently use.

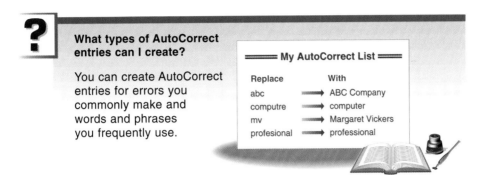

My AutoCorrect List

Replace	With
abc	ABC Company
compute	computer
mv	Margaret Vickers
profesional	professional

INSERT AN AUTOCORRECT ENTRY

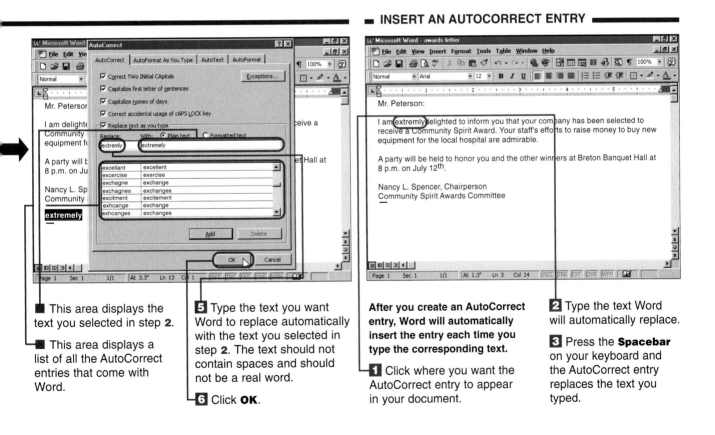

■ This area displays the text you selected in step **2**.

■ This area displays a list of all the AutoCorrect entries that come with Word.

5 Type the text you want Word to replace automatically with the text you selected in step **2**. The text should not contain spaces and should not be a real word.

6 Click **OK**.

After you create an AutoCorrect entry, Word will automatically insert the entry each time you type the corresponding text.

1 Click where you want the AutoCorrect entry to appear in your document.

2 Type the text Word will automatically replace.

3 Press the **Spacebar** on your keyboard and the AutoCorrect entry replaces the text you typed.

USING AUTOTEXT

To avoid typing the same text over and over again, you can store text you use frequently.

CREATE AN AUTOTEXT ENTRY

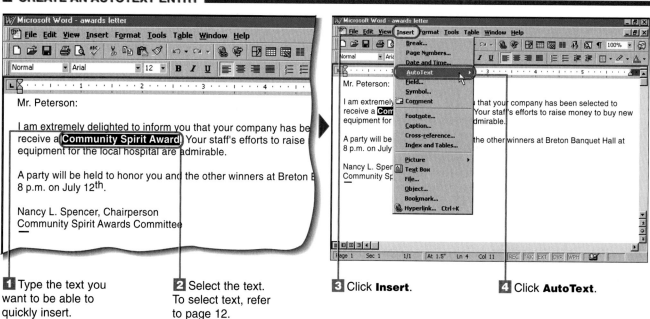

1 Type the text you want to be able to quickly insert.

2 Select the text. To select text, refer to page 12.

3 Click **Insert**.

4 Click **AutoText**.

What types of AutoText entries can I create?

You can create AutoText entries for text you plan to use often, such as a mailing address, product name, legal disclaimer or closing remark.

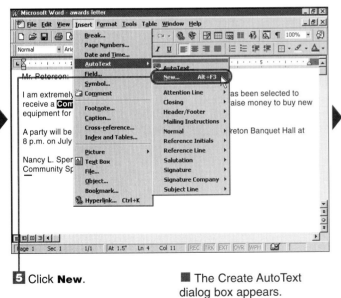

5 Click **New**.

■ The Create AutoText dialog box appears.

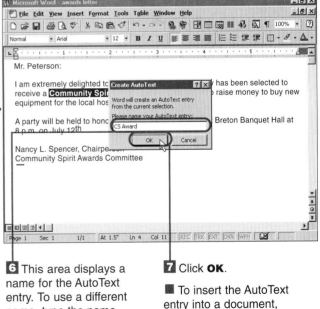

6 This area displays a name for the AutoText entry. To use a different name, type the name.

7 Click **OK**.

■ To insert the AutoText entry into a document, refer to page 82.

USING AUTOTEXT

After you create an AutoText entry, you can quickly insert the text into a document.

INSERT AN AUTOTEXT ENTRY

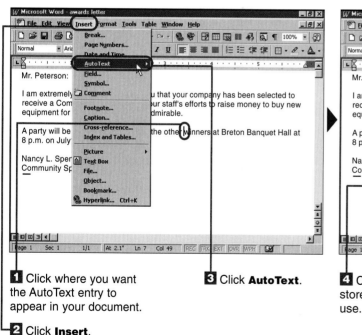

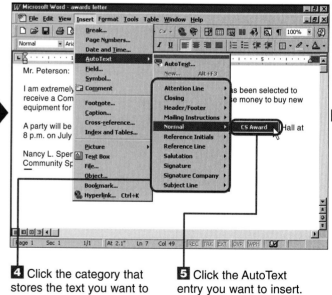

1 Click where you want the AutoText entry to appear in your document.

2 Click **Insert**.

3 Click **AutoText**.

4 Click the category that stores the text you want to use.

5 Click the AutoText entry you want to insert.

Does Word come with any AutoText entries?

Word comes with AutoText entries that can help you quickly create a letter. Some examples include:

Best wishes,
Thank you,
To Whom It May Concern:

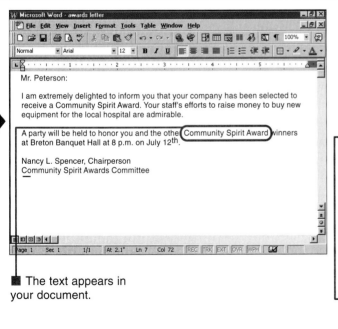

■ The text appears in your document.

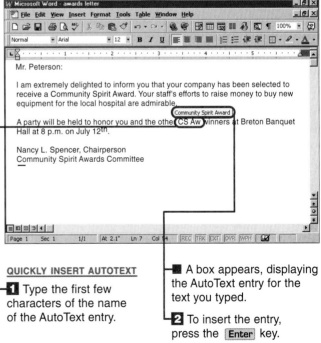

QUICKLY INSERT AUTOTEXT

1 Type the first few characters of the name of the AutoText entry.

■ A box appears, displaying the AutoText entry for the text you typed.

2 To insert the entry, press the **Enter** key.

Note: To ignore the AutoText entry, continue typing.

INSERT THE DATE AND TIME

You can have Word insert the current date and time in your document. Word will automatically update the information each time you print the document.

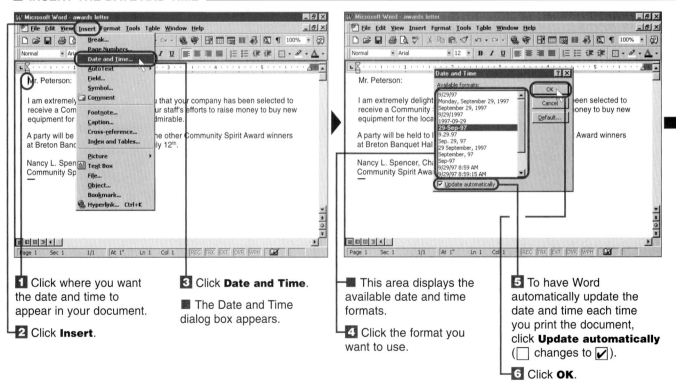

1 Click where you want the date and time to appear in your document.

2 Click **Insert**.

3 Click **Date and Time**.

■ The Date and Time dialog box appears.

■ This area displays the available date and time formats.

4 Click the format you want to use.

5 To have Word automatically update the date and time each time you print the document, click **Update automatically** (☐ changes to ☑).

6 Click **OK**.

Why did Word insert the wrong date and time in my document?

Word uses your computer's clock when adding the date and time to your documents.

If Word inserts the wrong date or time in your document, you must change the date or time set in your computer.

Note: For information on changing the date or time set in your computer, refer to your Windows manual.

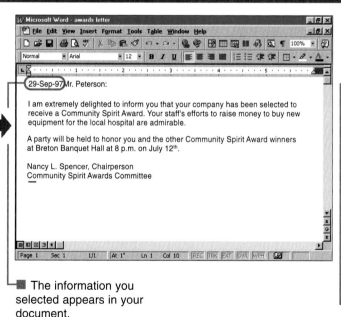

■ The information you selected appears in your document.

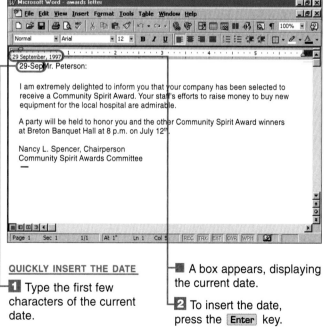

QUICKLY INSERT THE DATE

1 Type the first few characters of the current date.

■ A box appears, displaying the current date.

2 To insert the date, press the **Enter** key.

Note: If you do not want to insert the displayed date, continue typing.

COUNT WORDS IN A DOCUMENT

You can quickly determine the number of words in a document.

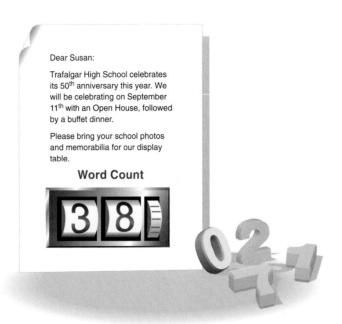

Dear Susan:

Trafalgar High School celebrates its 50th anniversary this year. We will be celebrating on September 11th with an Open House, followed by a buffet dinner.

Please bring your school photos and memorabilia for our display table.

Word Count

At the same time, you can determine the number of pages, characters, paragraphs and lines in the document.

■ COUNT WORDS IN A DOCUMENT

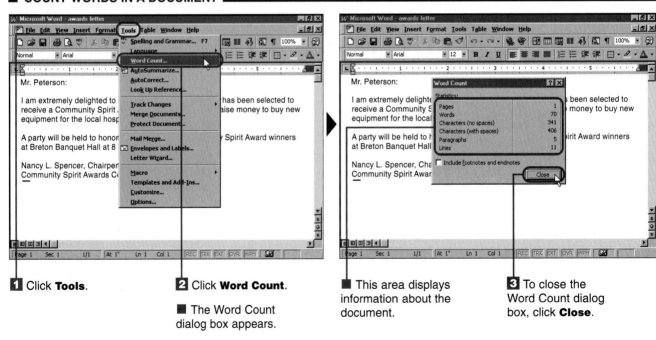

1 Click **Tools**.

2 Click **Word Count**.

■ The Word Count dialog box appears.

■ This area displays information about the document.

3 To close the Word Count dialog box, click **Close**.

DISPLAY NONPRINTING CHARACTERS

While you view and edit a document, you can display characters that will not appear on a printed page.

Displaying nonprinting characters helps you check for errors, such as extra spaces between words.

■ DISPLAY NONPRINTING CHARACTERS ■

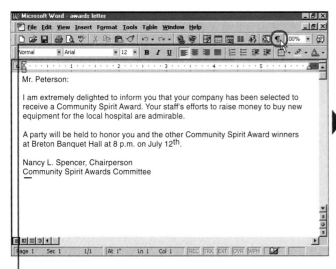

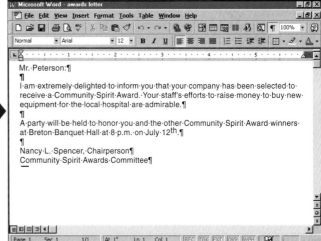

1 To display nonprinting characters in your document, click ¶.

■ Nonprinting characters appear in your document.

Examples include:

¶ Paragraph

· Space

→ Tab

■ To hide the characters, repeat step **1**.

ADD A COMMENT

You can add a comment to text in your document to make a note to yourself. You can easily view the comment later.

When you add a comment to text in your document, the text appears highlighted in yellow.

ADD A COMMENT

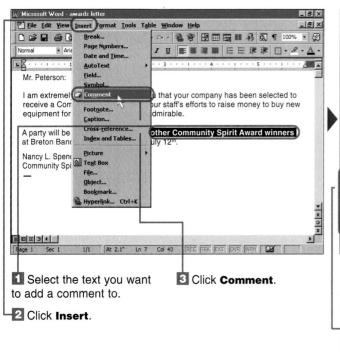

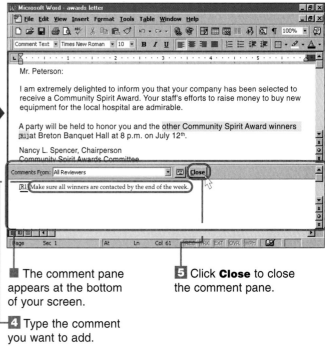

1 Select the text you want to add a comment to.

2 Click **Insert**.

3 Click **Comment**.

■ The comment pane appears at the bottom of your screen.

4 Type the comment you want to add.

5 Click **Close** to close the comment pane.

Why would I use comments in my documents?

Displaying comments in a document is helpful when you are reviewing a document. The highlighted text helps you instantly locate ideas that you want to review or verify in the document.

■ VIEW A COMMENT

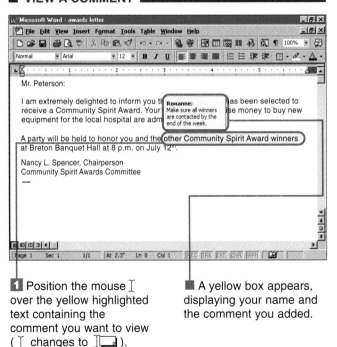

1 Position the mouse ⌶ over the yellow highlighted text containing the comment you want to view (⌶ changes to ⌶◻).

■ A yellow box appears, displaying your name and the comment you added.

■ REMOVE A COMMENT

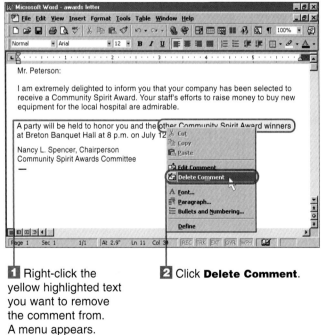

1 Right-click the yellow highlighted text you want to remove the comment from. A menu appears.

2 Click **Delete Comment**.

CHAPTER 6

Format Text

How can I emphasize information in my documents? This chapter will teach you many different ways to emphasize information so you can create interesting and attractive documents.

BOLD, ITALIC AND UNDERLINE

You can use the Bold, Italic and Underline features to emphasize information in your document.

■ BOLD, ITALIC AND UNDERLINE ■

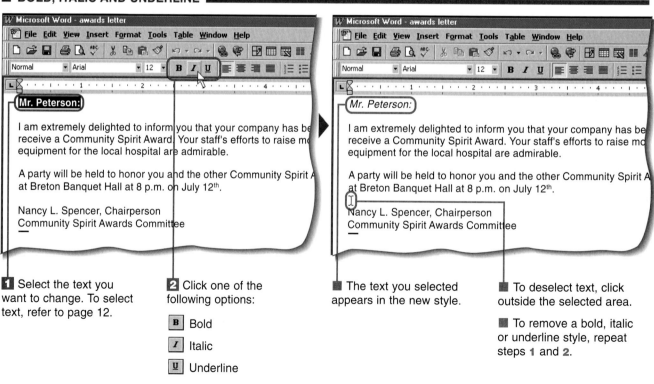

1 Select the text you want to change. To select text, refer to page 12.

2 Click one of the following options:

B	Bold
I	Italic
U	Underline

■ The text you selected appears in the new style.

■ To deselect text, click outside the selected area.

■ To remove a bold, italic or underline style, repeat steps **1** and **2**.

You can enhance the appearance of your document by aligning text in different ways.

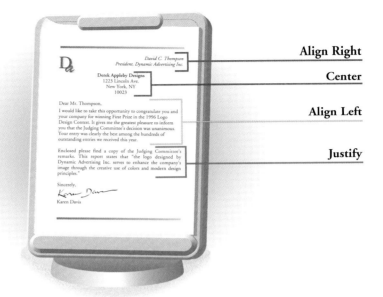

Align Right

Center

Align Left

Justify

CHANGE ALIGNMENT OF TEXT

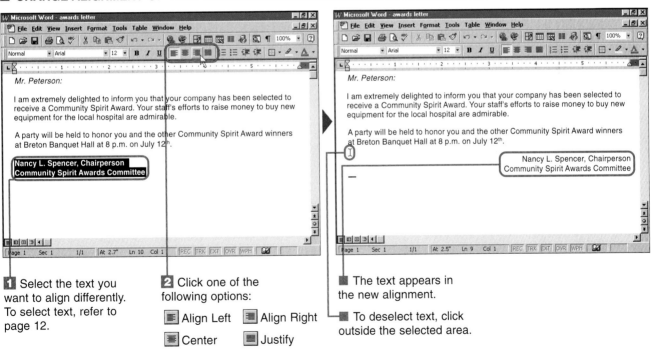

1 Select the text you want to align differently. To select text, refer to page 12.

2 Click one of the following options:

▤ Align Left ▤ Align Right

▤ Center ▤ Justify

■ The text appears in the new alignment.

■ To deselect text, click outside the selected area.

CHANGE FONT OF TEXT

You can enhance the appearance of your document by changing the design of the text.

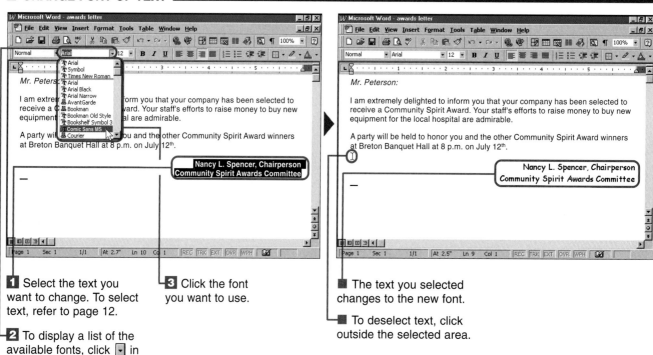

■ CHANGE FONT OF TEXT

1 Select the text you want to change. To select text, refer to page 12.

2 To display a list of the available fonts, click ▾ in this area.

3 Click the font you want to use.

■ The text you selected changes to the new font.

■ To deselect text, click outside the selected area.

You can increase or decrease the size of text in your document.

Word measures the size of text in points. There are 72 points in one inch.

Smaller text lets you fit more information on a page, but larger text is easier to read.

■ CHANGE SIZE OF TEXT

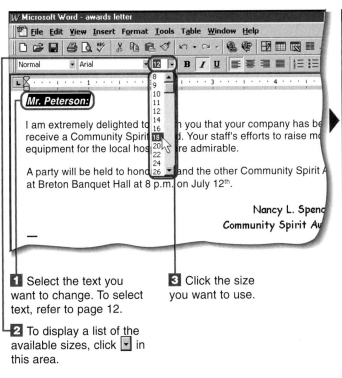

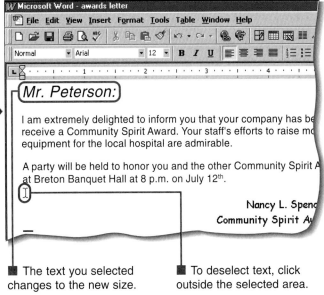

1 Select the text you want to change. To select text, refer to page 12.

2 To display a list of the available sizes, click ▾ in this area.

3 Click the size you want to use.

■ The text you selected changes to the new size.

■ To deselect text, click outside the selected area.

CHANGE TEXT COLOR

You can change the color of text to draw attention to headings or important information in your document.

■ CHANGE TEXT COLOR

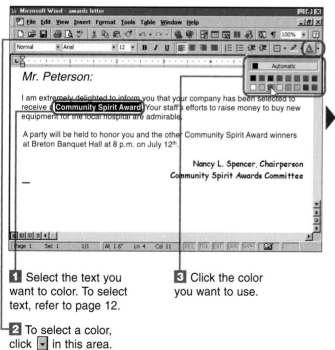

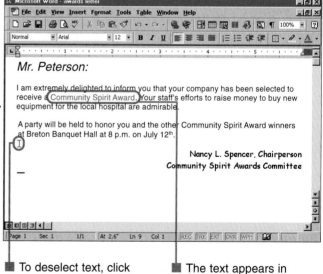

1 Select the text you want to color. To select text, refer to page 12.

2 To select a color, click ▾ in this area.

3 Click the color you want to use.

■ To deselect text, click outside the selected area.

■ The text appears in the color you selected.

REMOVE TEXT COLOR

■ To remove a color from text, repeat steps **1** to **3**, selecting **Automatic** in step **3**.

You can highlight important text in your document. Highlighting text is useful for marking text you want to verify later.

■ HIGHLIGHT TEXT

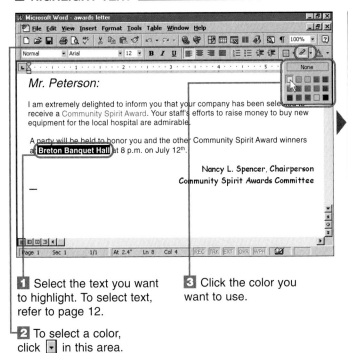

1 Select the text you want to highlight. To select text, refer to page 12.

2 To select a color, click ▾ in this area.

3 Click the color you want to use.

■ The text appears highlighted in the color you selected.

REMOVE HIGHLIGHT

■ To remove a highlight, repeat steps **1** to **3**, selecting **None** in step **3**.

CHANGE APPEARANCE OF TEXT

You can make text in your document look attractive by using various fonts, styles, sizes, underlines, colors and special effects.

CHANGE APPEARANCE OF TEXT

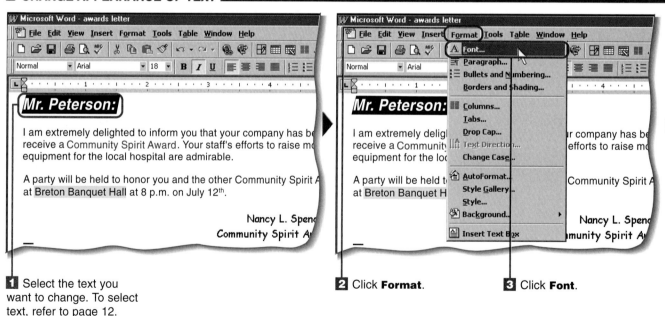

1 Select the text you want to change. To select text, refer to page 12.

2 Click **Format**.

3 Click **Font**.

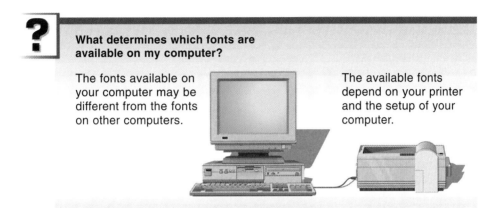

What determines which fonts are available on my computer?

The fonts available on your computer may be different from the fonts on other computers.

The available fonts depend on your printer and the setup of your computer.

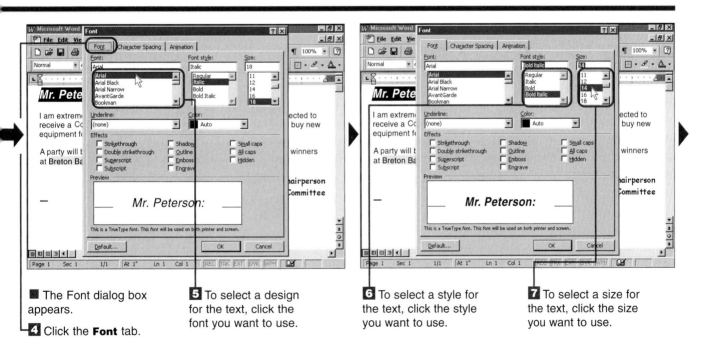

■ The Font dialog box appears.

4 Click the **Font** tab.

5 To select a design for the text, click the font you want to use.

6 To select a style for the text, click the style you want to use.

7 To select a size for the text, click the size you want to use.

CONTINUED

CHANGE APPEARANCE OF TEXT

Word offers many underline styles you can use to emphasize text in your document.

Single

Double

Dotted

Thick

Dash

Words only

Dot dash

Dot dot dash

Wave

■ CHANGE APPEARANCE OF TEXT (CONTINUED)

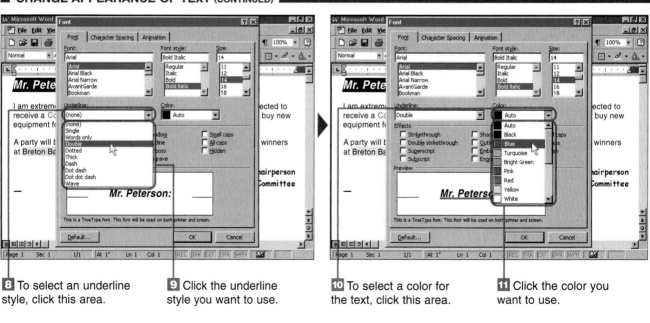

8 To select an underline style, click this area.

9 Click the underline style you want to use.

10 To select a color for the text, click this area.

11 Click the color you want to use.

What special effects can I add to my document?

Word offers many special effects.

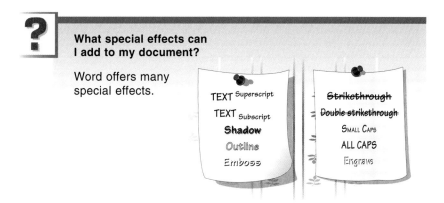

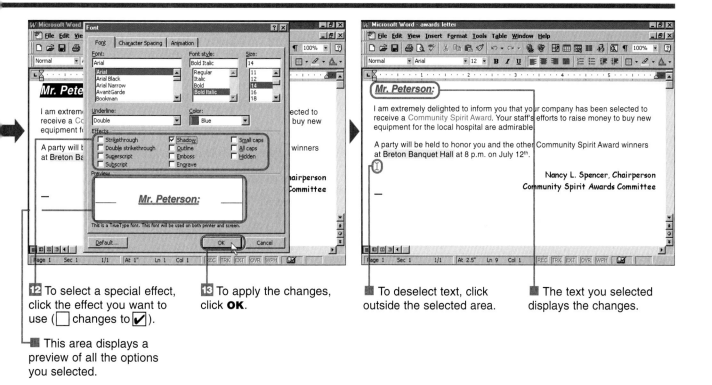

12 To select a special effect, click the effect you want to use (☐ changes to ☑).

■ This area displays a preview of all the options you selected.

13 To apply the changes, click **OK**.

■ To deselect text, click outside the selected area.

■ The text you selected displays the changes.

CHANGE FONT FOR ALL NEW DOCUMENTS

You can change the font that Word uses for every new document you create. This is useful if you want all of your future documents to appear in a specific font.

The font that Word uses for all new documents is called the default font.

■ CHANGE FONT FOR ALL NEW DOCUMENTS ■

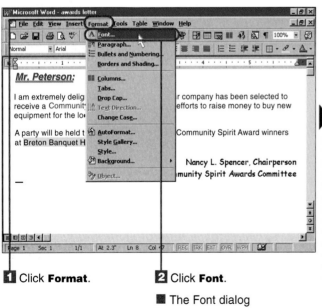

1 Click **Format**.

2 Click **Font**.

■ The Font dialog box appears.

3 Click the **Font** tab.

4 To select a design for the font you want to appear in all new documents, click the font you want to use.

5 To select a style, click the style you want to use.

6 To select a size, click the size you want to use.

Will changing the font for all new documents affect the documents I have already created?

No. To change the font of text in existing documents, refer to pages 98 to 101.

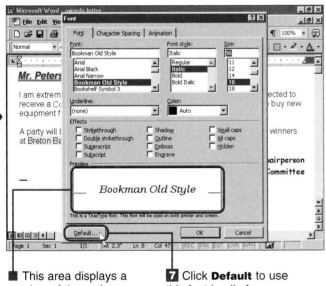

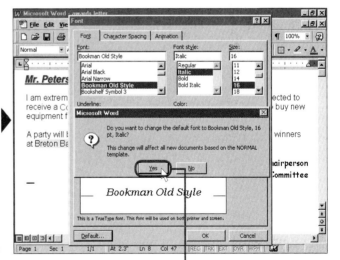

■ This area displays a preview of the options you selected.

7 Click **Default** to use this font in all of your new documents.

■ A dialog box appears, asking you to confirm the change.

8 Click **Yes** to confirm the change.

COPY FORMATTING

You can easily make one area of text look exactly like another.

COPY FORMATTING

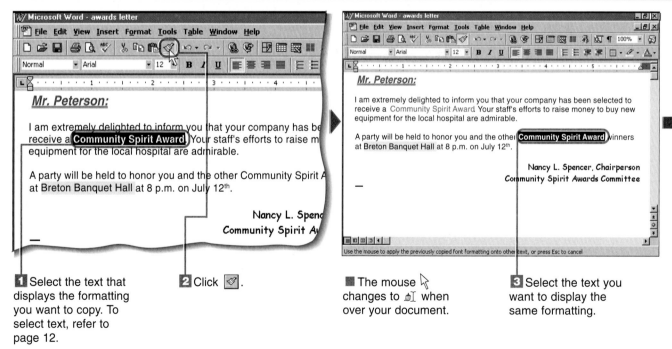

1 Select the text that displays the formatting you want to copy. To select text, refer to page 12.

2 Click 🖌.

■ The mouse ⟍ changes to ⟍I when over your document.

3 Select the text you want to display the same formatting.

Why would I want to copy the formatting of text?

You may want to copy the formatting of text to make all the headings or important words in your document look the same. This will give your document a consistent appearance.

You can copy formatting to several locations in your document.

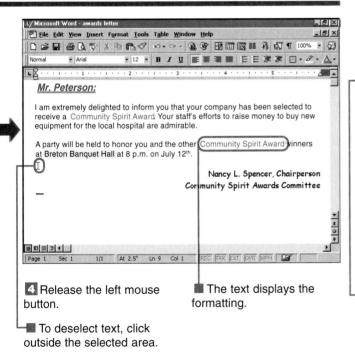

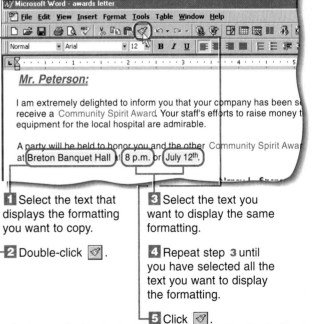

1 Select the text that displays the formatting you want to copy.

2 Double-click ✐.

3 Select the text you want to display the same formatting.

4 Repeat step **3** until you have selected all the text you want to display the formatting.

5 Click ✐.

4 Release the left mouse button.

■ To deselect text, click outside the selected area.

■ The text displays the formatting.

INSERT SYMBOLS

You can insert symbols that do not appear on your keyboard into your document.

INSERT SYMBOLS

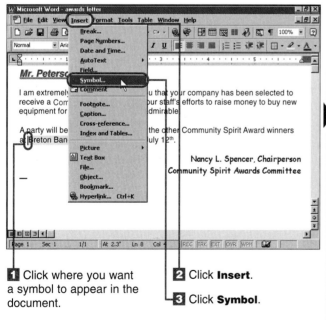

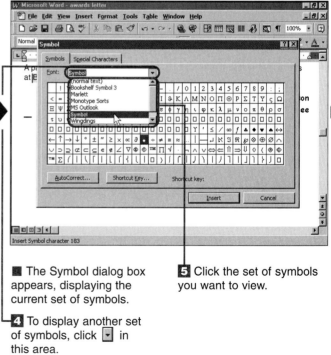

1 Click where you want a symbol to appear in the document.

2 Click **Insert**.

3 Click **Symbol**.

■ The Symbol dialog box appears, displaying the current set of symbols.

4 To display another set of symbols, click ▾ in this area.

5 Click the set of symbols you want to view.

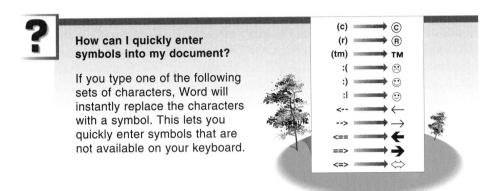

How can I quickly enter symbols into my document?

If you type one of the following sets of characters, Word will instantly replace the characters with a symbol. This lets you quickly enter symbols that are not available on your keyboard.

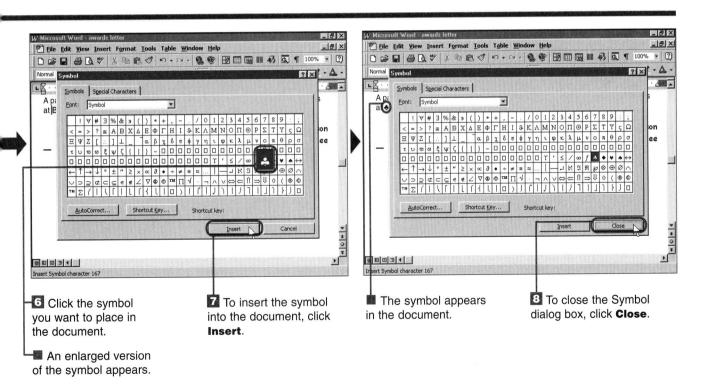

■ **6** Click the symbol you want to place in the document.

■ An enlarged version of the symbol appears.

7 To insert the symbol into the document, click **Insert**.

■ The symbol appears in the document.

8 To close the Symbol dialog box, click **Close**.

CHANGE SPACING BETWEEN CHARACTERS

You can alter the look
of text by changing
the spacing between
characters.

Expanding the spacing can
give headings a special look.
You can condense the spacing
if you want to fit more text on
a line in your document.

■ CHANGE SPACING BETWEEN CHARACTERS ■

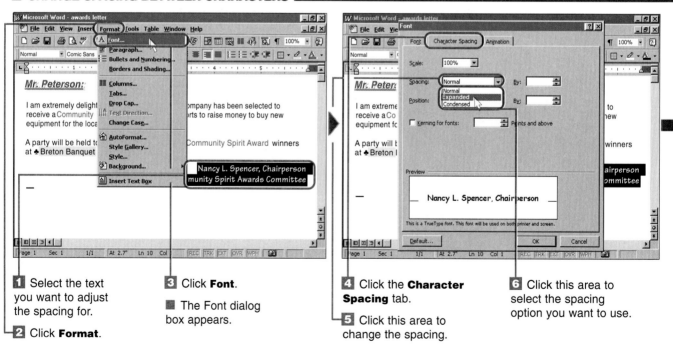

1 Select the text
you want to adjust
the spacing for.

2 Click **Format**.

3 Click **Font**.

■ The Font dialog
box appears.

4 Click the **Character
Spacing** tab.

5 Click this area to
change the spacing.

6 Click this area to
select the spacing
option you want to use.

Can I change the spacing between characters for all the text in a paragraph?

You can change the spacing between characters for any amount of text. When you change the spacing between characters, the spacing between words also changes.

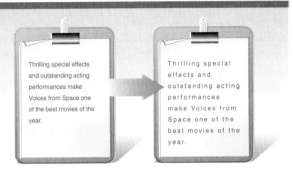

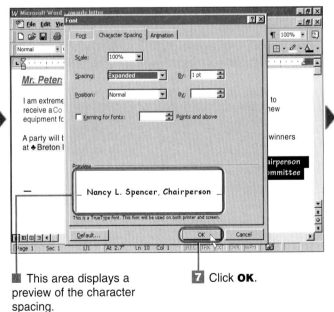

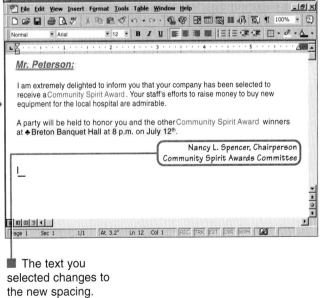

■ This area displays a preview of the character spacing.

7 Click **OK**.

■ The text you selected changes to the new spacing.

fresh
reel

1.5

CHAPTER 7

Format Paragraphs

Are you wondering how to change line spacing and indent paragraphs in your documents? Would you like to add a border or create a drop cap? Find out how in this chapter.

CHANGE LINE SPACING

You can change the amount of
space between the lines of text
in your document to make your
document easier to review
and edit.

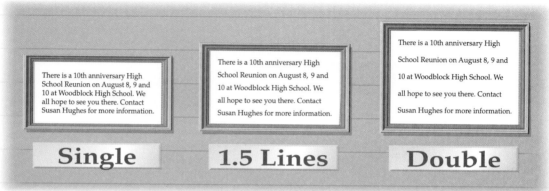

CHANGE LINE SPACING

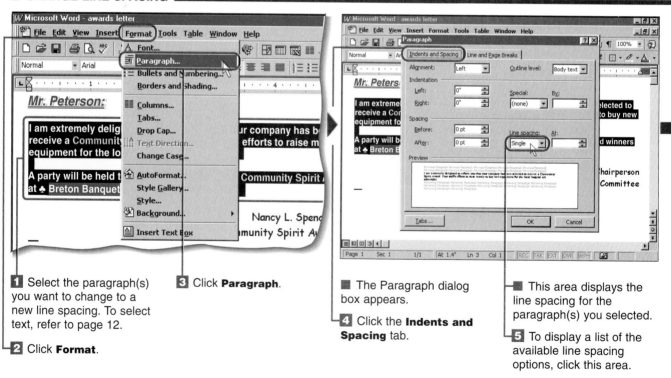

1 Select the paragraph(s)
you want to change to a
new line spacing. To select
text, refer to page 12.

2 Click **Format**.

3 Click **Paragraph**.

■ The Paragraph dialog
box appears.

4 Click the **Indents and
Spacing** tab.

■ This area displays the
line spacing for the
paragraph(s) you selected.

5 To display a list of the
available line spacing
options, click this area.

Does Word ever automatically adjust the line spacing?

Word automatically increases the spacing of lines that contain large characters.

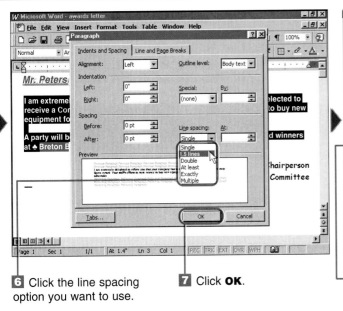

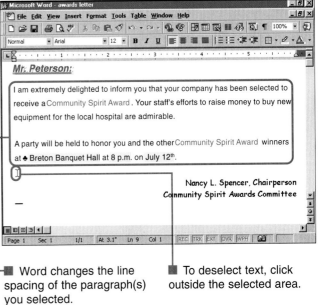

6 Click the line spacing option you want to use.

7 Click **OK**.

■ Word changes the line spacing of the paragraph(s) you selected.

■ To deselect text, click outside the selected area.

INDENT PARAGRAPHS

You can use the Indent feature to set off paragraphs in your document.

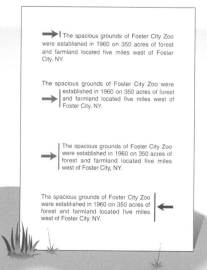

Indent first line

Indent all but first line

Indent all lines

Indent right edge of all lines

■ INDENT PARAGRAPHS

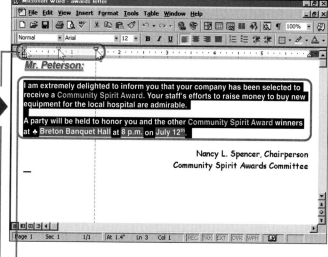

■ These symbols let you indent the left edge of a paragraph:

▽ Indent first line

△ Indent all but first line

▢ Indent all lines

■ This symbol (△) lets you indent the right edge of all lines.

Note: If the ruler is not displayed on the screen, refer to page 43 to display the ruler.

1 Select the paragraph(s) you want to indent. To select text, refer to page 12.

2 Drag the indent symbol to a new position.

■ A line shows the new indent position.

?

What is a hanging indent?

A hanging indent moves all but the first line of a paragraph to the right. Hanging indents are useful when you are creating a résumé, glossary or bibliography.

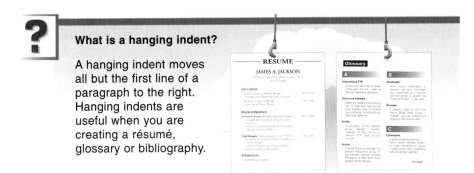

QUICKLY INDENT ALL LINES IN A PARAGRAPH

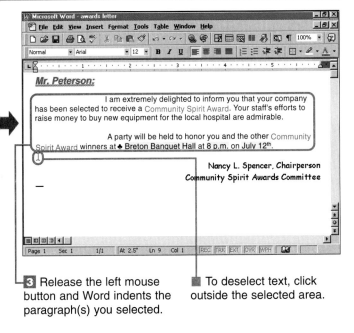

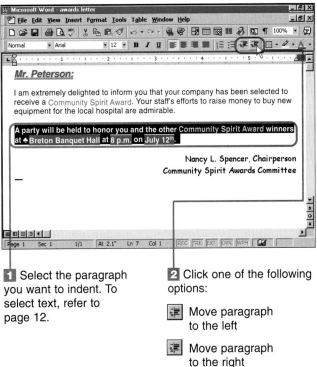

3 Release the left mouse button and Word indents the paragraph(s) you selected.

■ To deselect text, click outside the selected area.

1 Select the paragraph you want to indent. To select text, refer to page 12.

2 Click one of the following options:

▨ Move paragraph to the left

▨ Move paragraph to the right

CHANGE TAB SETTINGS

You can use tabs to line up columns of information in your document. Word offers four types of tabs.

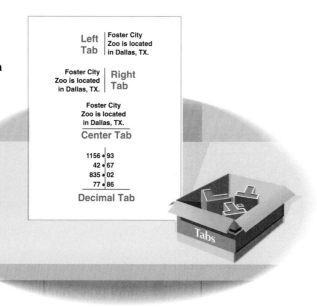

Word automatically places a tab every 0.5 inches across each page.

ADD A TAB

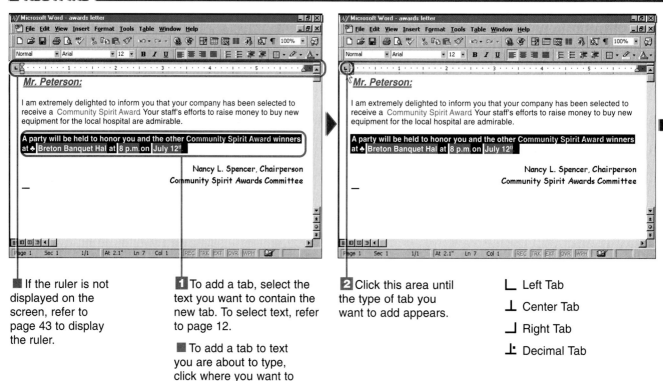

■ If the ruler is not displayed on the screen, refer to page 43 to display the ruler.

1 To add a tab, select the text you want to contain the new tab. To select text, refer to page 12.

■ To add a tab to text you are about to type, click where you want to type the text.

2 Click this area until the type of tab you want to add appears.

L Left Tab

⊥ Center Tab

⅃ Right Tab

⊥· Decimal Tab

What happens if I use spaces instead of tabs to line up columns of text?

Your document may not print correctly if you use spaces instead of tabs to line up columns of text.

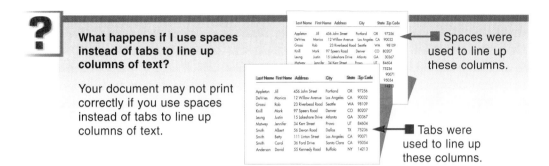

■ Spaces were used to line up these columns.

■ Tabs were used to line up these columns.

USING TABS

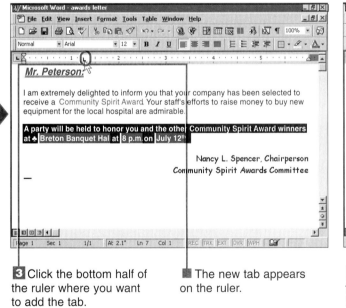

3 Click the bottom half of the ruler where you want to add the tab.

■ The new tab appears on the ruler.

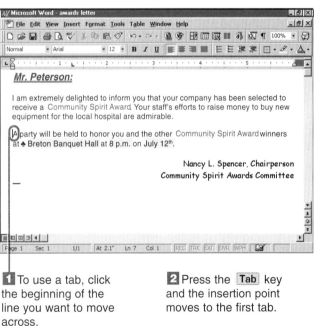

1 To use a tab, click the beginning of the line you want to move across.

2 Press the Tab key and the insertion point moves to the first tab.

CHANGE TAB SETTINGS

You can easily move a tab to a different position on the ruler.

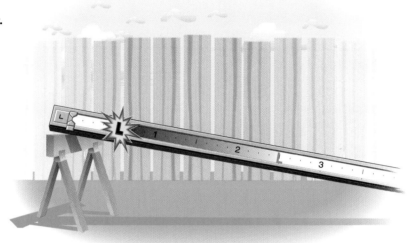

■ MOVE A TAB ■

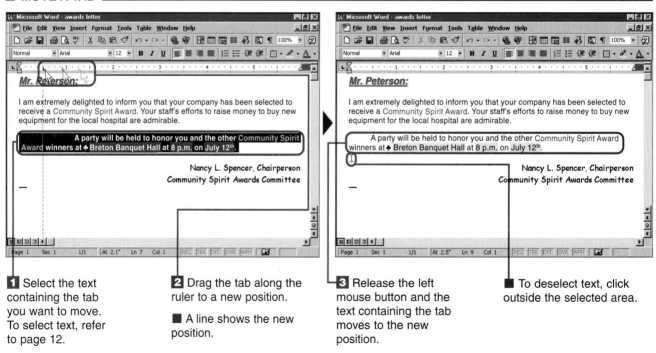

1 Select the text containing the tab you want to move. To select text, refer to page 12.

2 Drag the tab along the ruler to a new position.

■ A line shows the new position.

3 Release the left mouse button and the text containing the tab moves to the new position.

■ To deselect text, click outside the selected area.

When you no longer need a tab, you can remove it from the ruler.

■ REMOVE A TAB

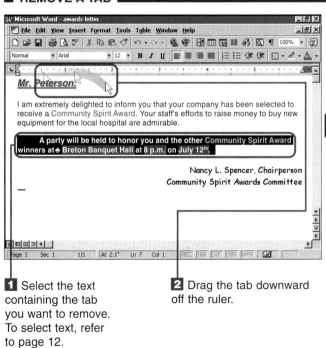

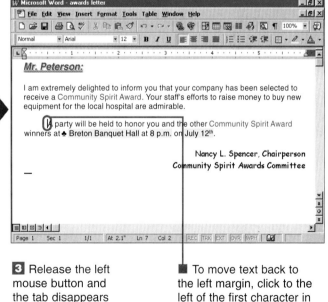

1 Select the text containing the tab you want to remove. To select text, refer to page 12.

2 Drag the tab downward off the ruler.

3 Release the left mouse button and the tab disappears from the ruler.

■ To move text back to the left margin, click to the left of the first character in the paragraph. Then press the **◆Backspace** key.

CHANGE TAB SETTINGS

You can insert a line or row of dots before a tab to help lead the eye from one column of information to another.

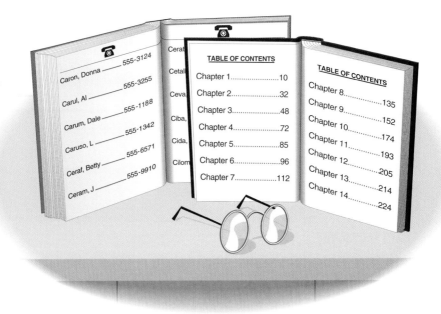

■ ADD A TAB WITH LEADER CHARACTERS ■

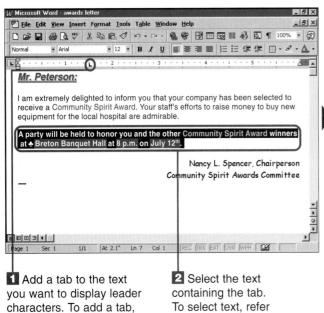

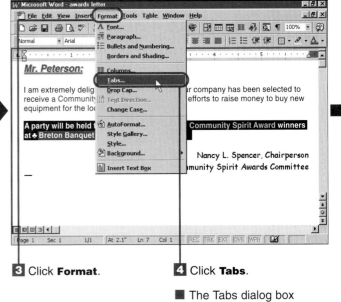

1 Add a tab to the text you want to display leader characters. To add a tab, refer to page 116.

2 Select the text containing the tab. To select text, refer to page 12.

Note: You can also add a tab to text you are about to type.

3 Click **Format**.

4 Click **Tabs**.

■ The Tabs dialog box appears.

Why would I use leader characters?

Leader characters make information such as a table of contents or a list of telephone numbers easier to read.

Leader characters are also used in forms to create areas where people can enter information.

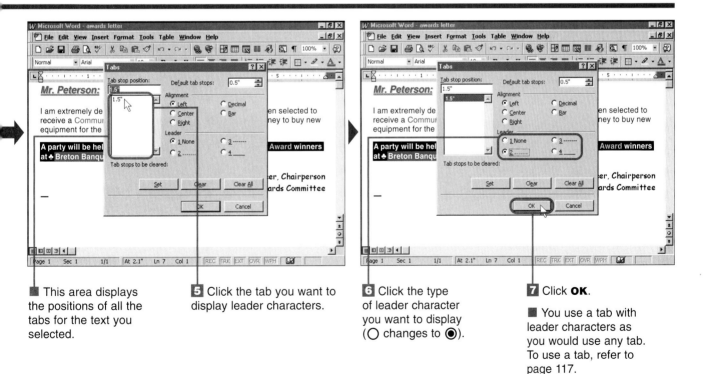

■ This area displays the positions of all the tabs for the text you selected.

5 Click the tab you want to display leader characters.

6 Click the type of leader character you want to display (○ changes to ●).

7 Click **OK**.

■ You use a tab with leader characters as you would use any tab. To use a tab, refer to page 117.

ADD BULLETS OR NUMBERS

You can separate items in a list by beginning each item with a bullet or number.

■ ADD BULLETS OR NUMBERS

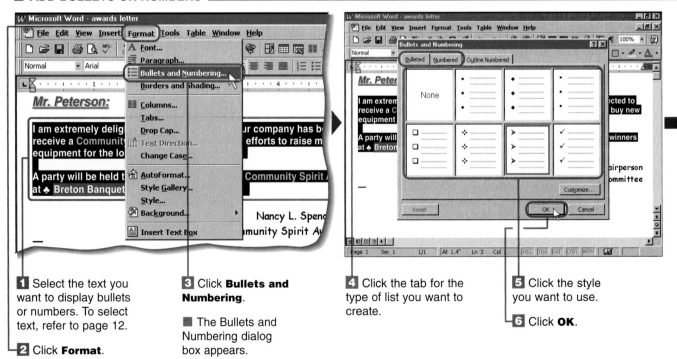

1 Select the text you want to display bullets or numbers. To select text, refer to page 12.

2 Click **Format**.

3 Click **Bullets and Numbering**.

■ The Bullets and Numbering dialog box appears.

4 Click the tab for the type of list you want to create.

5 Click the style you want to use.

6 Click **OK**.

Should I use bullets or numbers in my list?

Bullets are useful for items in no particular order, such as a shopping list.

Shopping List:
- eggs
- butter
- milk
- lettuce
- tomatoes

Recipe:
1. Preheat oven to 300°F
2. Grate 1 cup of cheese
3. Dice 1/4 cup of onions
4. Slice 1/2 a red pepper into strips
5. Add cheese, onions and red pepper to meat sauce
6. Bake for 20 minutes

Numbers are useful for items in a specific order, such as a recipe.

ADD BULLETS OR NUMBERS AS YOU TYPE

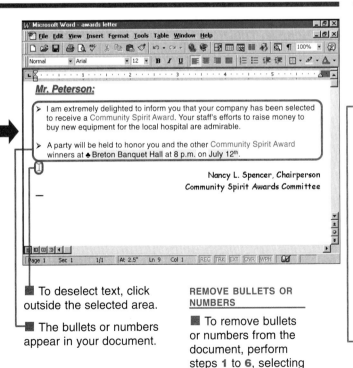

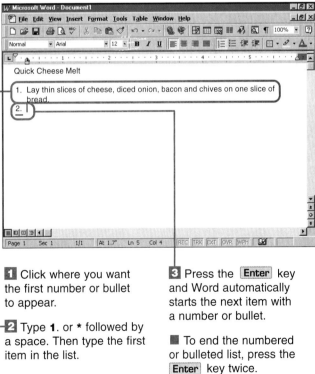

■ To deselect text, click outside the selected area.

■ The bullets or numbers appear in your document.

REMOVE BULLETS OR NUMBERS

■ To remove bullets or numbers from the document, perform steps **1** to **6**, selecting **None** in step **5**.

1 Click where you want the first number or bullet to appear.

2 Type **1.** or ***** followed by a space. Then type the first item in the list.

3 Press the **Enter** key and Word automatically starts the next item with a number or bullet.

■ To end the numbered or bulleted list, press the **Enter** key twice.

ADD A BORDER

You can add a border to emphasize an area of text in your document.

ADD A BORDER

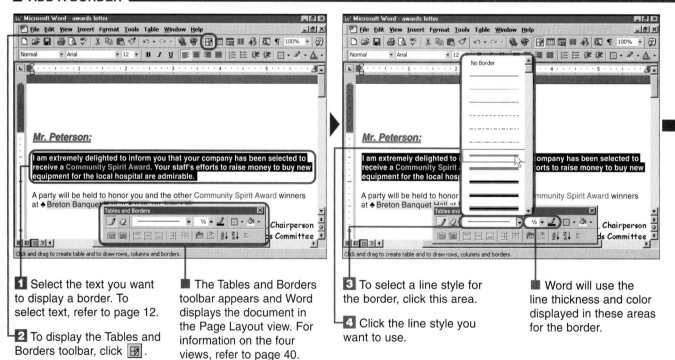

1 Select the text you want to display a border. To select text, refer to page 12.

2 To display the Tables and Borders toolbar, click 🔠.

■ The Tables and Borders toolbar appears and Word displays the document in the Page Layout view. For information on the four views, refer to page 40.

3 To select a line style for the border, click this area.

4 Click the line style you want to use.

■ Word will use the line thickness and color displayed in these areas for the border.

How can I quickly add a line across my document?

If you type one of the sets of characters in this chart and then press the ⬚ **Enter** ⬚ key, Word will instantly add a line across your document.

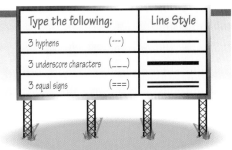

Type the following:		Line Style
3 hyphens	(---)	————————
3 underscore characters	(___)	————————
3 equal signs	(===)	═══════════

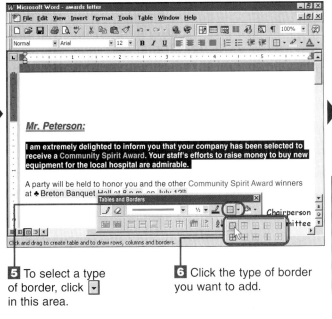

5 To select a type of border, click ⬇ in this area.

6 Click the type of border you want to add.

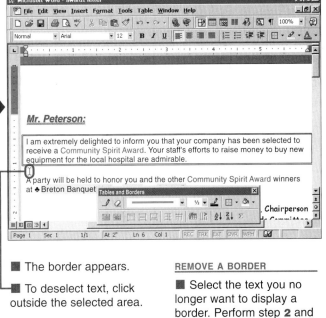

■ The border appears.

■ To deselect text, click outside the selected area.

■ To hide the Tables and Borders toolbar, repeat step **2**.

REMOVE A BORDER

■ Select the text you no longer want to display a border. Perform step **2** and then perform steps **5** and **6**, selecting ⬚ in step **6**.

ADD SHADING

You can emphasize an area of text in your document by adding shading.

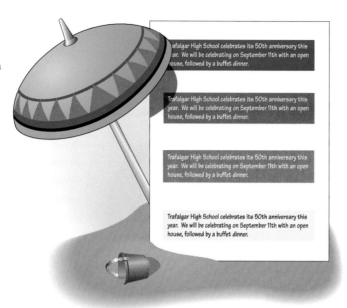

ADD SHADING

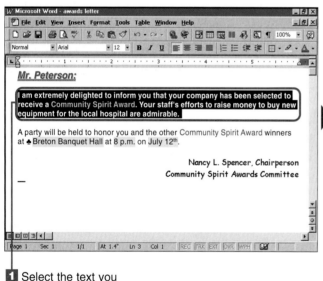

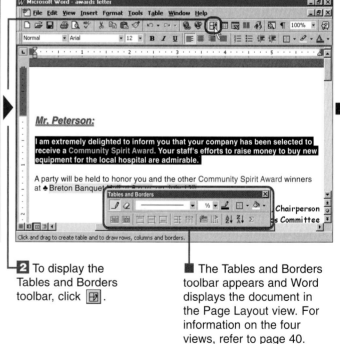

1 Select the text you want to display shading. To select text, refer to page 12.

2 To display the Tables and Borders toolbar, click 🖽.

■ The Tables and Borders toolbar appears and Word displays the document in the Page Layout view. For information on the four views, refer to page 40.

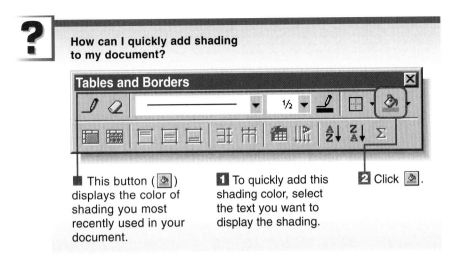

How can I quickly add shading to my document?

■ This button (⬛) displays the color of shading you most recently used in your document.

1 To quickly add this shading color, select the text you want to display the shading.

2 Click ⬛.

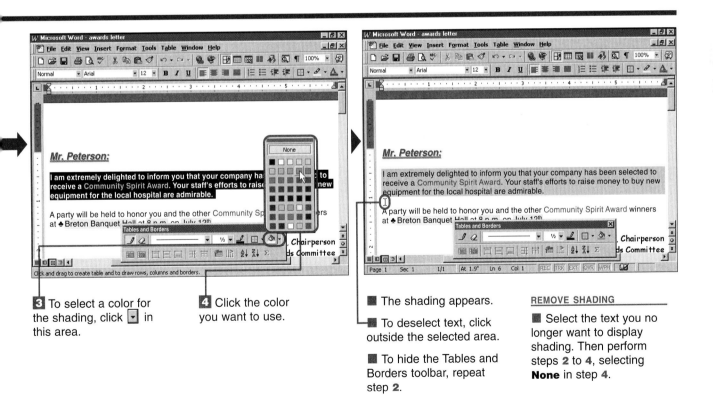

3 To select a color for the shading, click ▾ in this area.

4 Click the color you want to use.

■ The shading appears.

■ To deselect text, click outside the selected area.

■ To hide the Tables and Borders toolbar, repeat step **2**.

REMOVE SHADING

■ Select the text you no longer want to display shading. Then perform steps **2** to **4**, selecting **None** in step **4**.

CREATE A DROP CAP

You can create a large first letter at the beginning of a paragraph. Drop caps help draw attention to important sections of a document.

Word offers two drop cap styles that you can use:

Dropped

In Margin

■ CREATE A DROP CAP ■

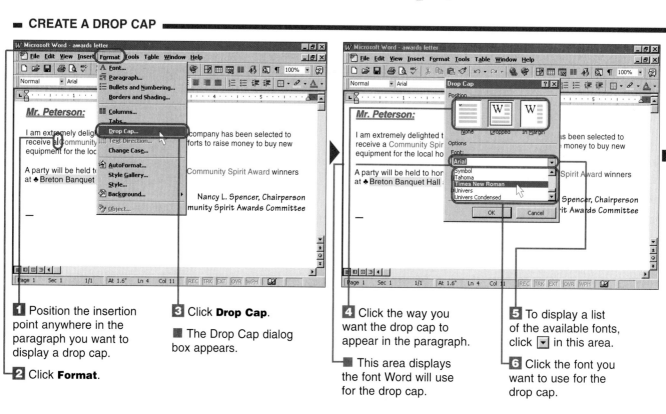

1 Position the insertion point anywhere in the paragraph you want to display a drop cap.

2 Click **Format**.

3 Click **Drop Cap**.

■ The Drop Cap dialog box appears.

4 Click the way you want the drop cap to appear in the paragraph.

■ This area displays the font Word will use for the drop cap.

5 To display a list of the available fonts, click ▼ in this area.

6 Click the font you want to use for the drop cap.

Can I create a drop cap using more than one letter?

You can create a drop cap using multiple characters or even an entire word at the beginning of a paragraph.

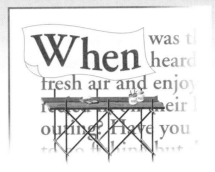

■ Select the characters or word you want to create the drop cap for and then perform steps **2** to **9** below.

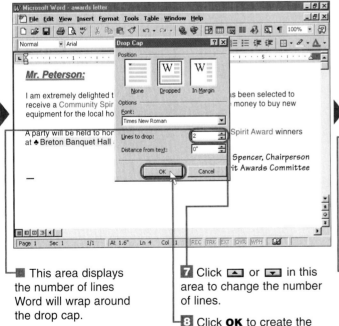

■ This area displays the number of lines Word will wrap around the drop cap.

7 Click ▲ or ▼ in this area to change the number of lines.

8 Click **OK** to create the drop cap in your document.

■ The drop cap appears in your document. Word displays the document in the Page Layout view. For information on the four views, refer to page 40.

9 To deselect the drop cap, click outside the drop cap area.

REMOVE A DROP CAP

■ Position the insertion point anywhere in the paragraph you no longer want to display a drop cap. Perform steps **2** to **4**, selecting **None** in step **4**. Then perform step **8**.

HYPHENATE TEXT

You can have Word automatically add hyphens where needed in your document. Hyphenating text can help save space in your document by eliminating gaps at the ends of the lines.

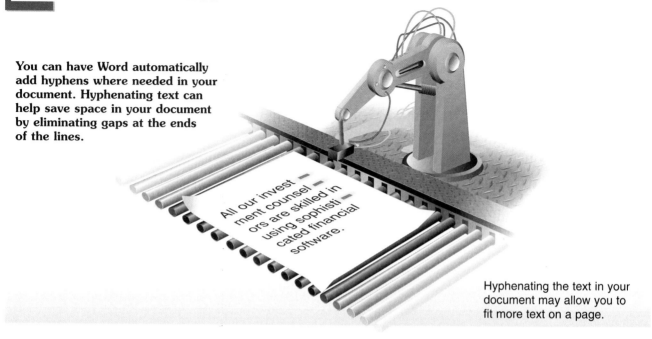

Hyphenating the text in your document may allow you to fit more text on a page.

■ HYPHENATE TEXT

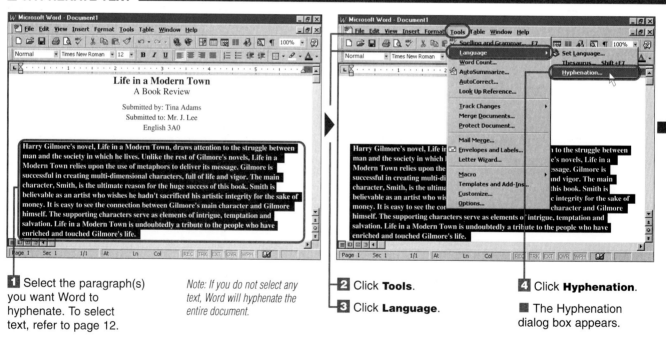

1 Select the paragraph(s) you want Word to hyphenate. To select text, refer to page 12.

Note: If you do not select any text, Word will hyphenate the entire document.

2 Click **Tools**.

3 Click **Language**.

4 Click **Hyphenation**.

■ The Hyphenation dialog box appears.

? **What will happen to the hyphenation in my document if I later edit the text?**

If you later add or delete text in the document, Word will automatically adjust the hyphenation for you.

All of our investment counsel‑ ors are skilled in using so‑ phisticated financial software. People who have an entre‑ preneurial spirit will find our services to be very useful.

All of Macmillan Inc.'s invest‑ ment counselors are skilled in using the most highly sophis‑ ticated financial software. People with an entrepreneu‑ rial spirit will find our services to be very useful.

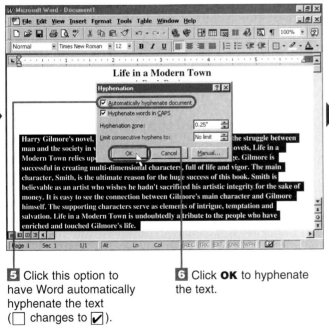

5 Click this option to have Word automatically hyphenate the text (☐ changes to ☑).

6 Click **OK** to hyphenate the text.

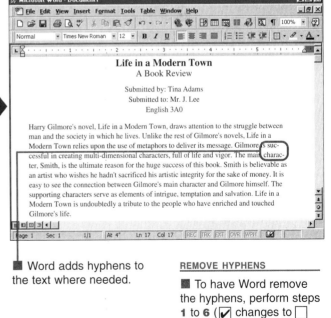

■ Word adds hyphens to the text where needed.

REMOVE HYPHENS

■ To have Word remove the hyphens, perform steps **1** to **6** (☑ changes to ☐ in step **5**).

The Olympic Flame

One constant that remains from ancient times, is the Olympic flame. It has remained since the beginning.

In ancient times the Olympic games took on a very religious significance. Olympia, the grounds on which the first games were played, was considered sacred.

The ancient Greeks believed very deeply in a relationship between life and death and the connection that existed between religion and burial traditions. For them, the Olympic flame. Therefore, each time the ancient Olympic games were held, the Olympic flame was lit to symbolize the re-birth of the spirit of their dead heroes.

Today, that tradition continues. In 1936, for the first time in modern Olympic history, the sacred Olympic flame was carried to Berlin, Germany where the 11th Olympiad took place. Since that time and to this present day, runners, through a relay, transport the flame, from Greece, every four years to the that is to host the Olympics. runner, carrying the into the stadium at opening Olympic ceremony and lights the Olympic torch which burns throughout games until it is extinguished during the closing ceremony

Format Pages

Unsure of how to format your pages to include such things as footnotes or columns? Confused by changing your margins or paper size? Do not be intimidated—Word allows you to use many sophisticated formatting options with ease.

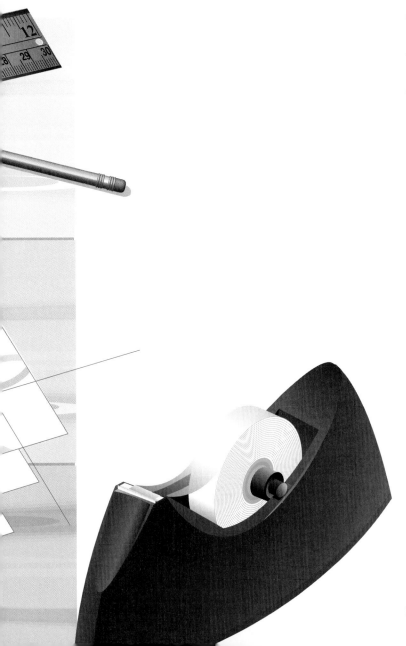

ADD PAGE NUMBERS

You can have Word
number the pages in
your document.

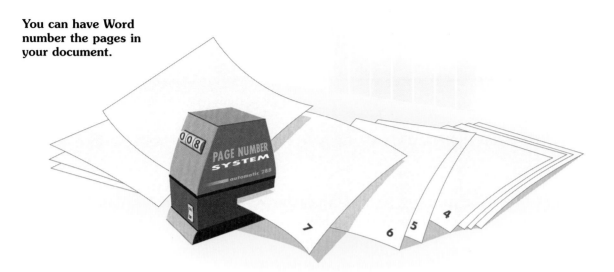

■ ADD PAGE NUMBERS ■

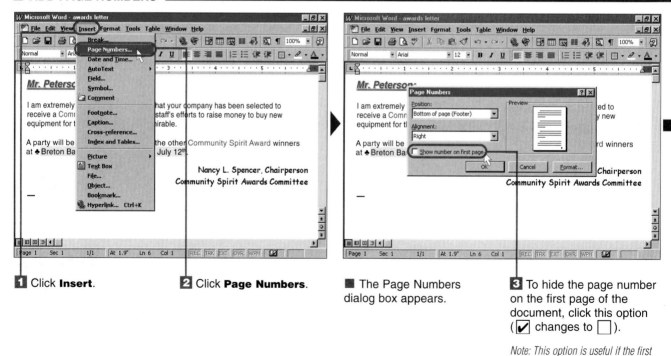

1 Click **Insert**.

2 Click **Page Numbers**.

■ The Page Numbers
dialog box appears.

3 To hide the page number
on the first page of the
document, click this option
(☑ changes to ☐).

*Note: This option is useful if the first
page of the document is a title page.*

Will Word adjust the page numbers if I make changes to my document?

If you add, remove or rearrange text in your document, Word will automatically adjust the page numbers for you.

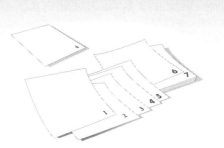

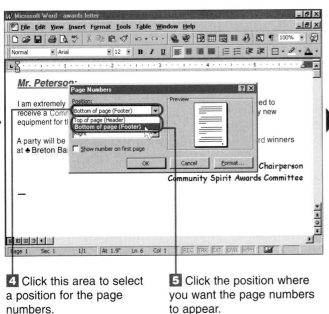

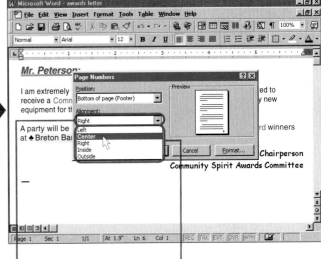

4 Click this area to select a position for the page numbers.

5 Click the position where you want the page numbers to appear.

6 Click this area to select an alignment for the page numbers.

7 Click the alignment you want to use.

CONTINUED

ADD PAGE NUMBERS

Word offers several formats you can use for your page numbers. You can choose the format that best suits your document.

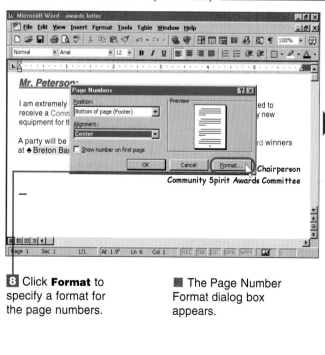

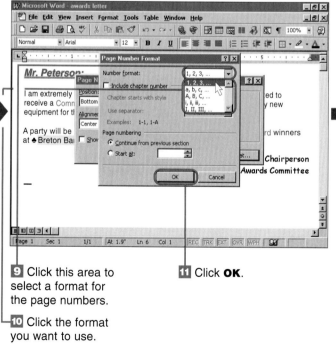

8 Click **Format** to specify a format for the page numbers.

■ The Page Number Format dialog box appears.

9 Click this area to select a format for the page numbers.

10 Click the format you want to use.

11 Click **OK**.

How do I delete page numbers from my document?

When you add page numbers, Word inserts the page numbers in the document's header or footer. To remove the page numbers, you must delete the page number from the header or footer.

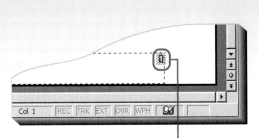

1 Display the headers and footers in your document. To display headers and footers, refer to page 138.

2 Double-click the page number.

3 Press the Delete key to remove the page number.

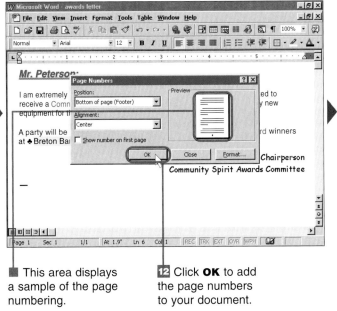

■ This area displays a sample of the page numbering.

12 Click **OK** to add the page numbers to your document.

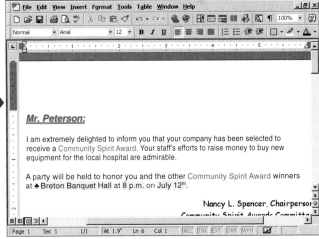

■ The document displays the page numbers.

Note: If the page numbers do not appear, you must change to the Page Layout view. To change to the Page Layout view, refer to page 40.

ADD A HEADER AND FOOTER

You can add a header and footer to each page of your document.

■ A header appears at the top of each page.

■ A footer appears at the bottom of each page.

■ ADD A HEADER AND FOOTER (To Every Page) ■

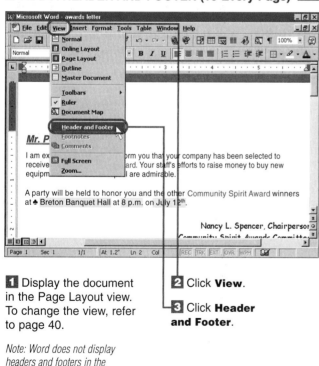

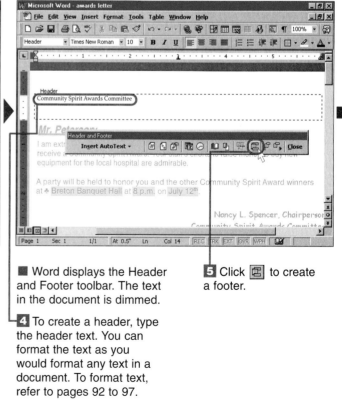

1 Display the document in the Page Layout view. To change the view, refer to page 40.

Note: Word does not display headers and footers in the Normal view.

2 Click **View**.

3 Click **Header and Footer**.

■ Word displays the Header and Footer toolbar. The text in the document is dimmed.

4 To create a header, type the header text. You can format the text as you would format any text in a document. To format text, refer to pages 92 to 97.

5 Click 🖾 to create a footer.

?

What information can a header or footer contain?

A header or footer can contain information such as the company name, author's name, chapter title or date.

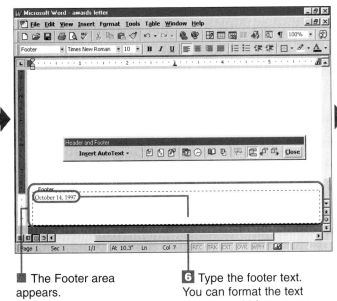

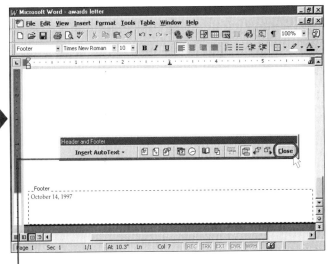

■ The Footer area appears.

Note: You can return to the header area at any time by repeating step 5.

6 Type the footer text. You can format the text as you would format any text in a document.

7 When you have finished creating the header and footer, click **Close**.

EDIT A HEADER OR FOOTER

1 To edit a header or footer, repeat steps **1** to **7**.

ADD A HEADER AND FOOTER

You can have different headers and footers on different pages in your document.

■ **ADD A HEADER AND FOOTER (Vary Within Document)**

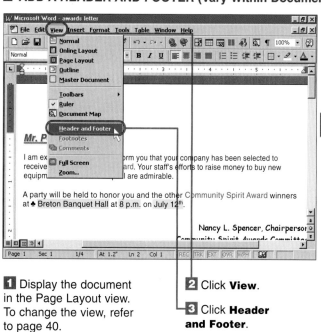

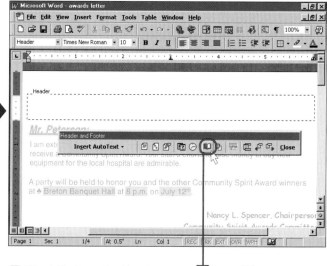

1 Display the document in the Page Layout view. To change the view, refer to page 40.

Note: Word does not display headers and footers in the Normal view.

2 Click **View**.

3 Click **Header and Footer**.

■ Word displays the Header and Footer toolbar. The text in the document is dimmed.

4 Click 🔲 to set up different headers and footers for different pages in the document.

■ The Page Setup dialog box appears.

What header and footer areas does Word provide?

First Page Header/Footer

The text you type in this area only appears on the first page of the document.

Note: If you do not want a header or footer on the first page, leave this area blank.

Odd Page Header/Footer

The text you type in this area appears on each odd-numbered page in the document.

Header/Footer

The text you type in this area appears on all but the first page of the document.

Even Page Header/Footer

The text you type in this area appears on each even-numbered page in the document.

Note: The available areas depend on the option(s) you selected in steps 5 and 6 below.

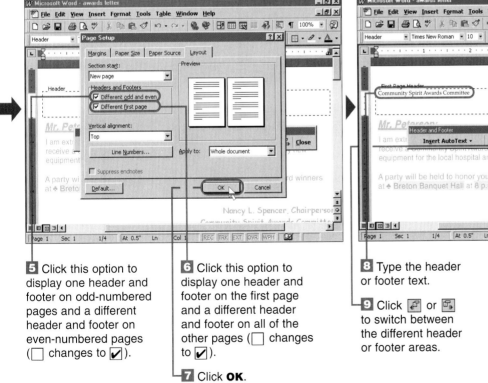

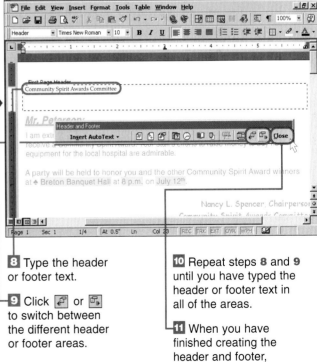

5 Click this option to display one header and footer on odd-numbered pages and a different header and footer on even-numbered pages (☐ changes to ✔).

6 Click this option to display one header and footer on the first page and a different header and footer on all of the other pages (☐ changes to ✔).

7 Click **OK**.

8 Type the header or footer text.

9 Click 🖳 or 🖳 to switch between the different header or footer areas.

10 Repeat steps 8 and 9 until you have typed the header or footer text in all of the areas.

11 When you have finished creating the header and footer, click **Close**.

ADD FOOTNOTES

A footnote appears at the
bottom of a page to provide
additional information
about text in your
document.

1 H Smith, Aeronautical Refrigeration Repair
(California: Quest Publishing, 1989) 10.

2 R. Anderson, Volatile Cold Gases
(Alaska: Inert Publishing, 199

Word ensures that the
footnote text always
appears on the same
page as the footnote
number.

ADD FOOTNOTES

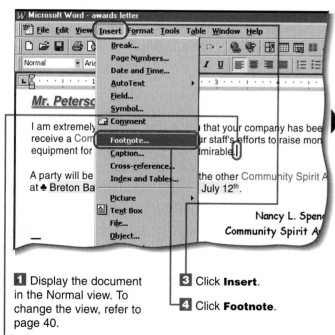

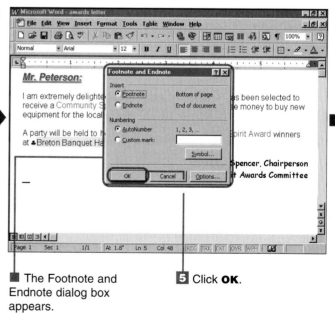

1 Display the document
in the Normal view. To
change the view, refer to
page 40.

2 Click where you want
the number of the footnote
to appear.

3 Click **Insert**.

4 Click **Footnote**.

■ The Footnote and
Endnote dialog box
appears.

5 Click **OK**.

Will Word adjust the footnote numbers if I add or remove footnotes?

If you add or remove footnotes in your document, Word will automatically renumber the footnotes for you.

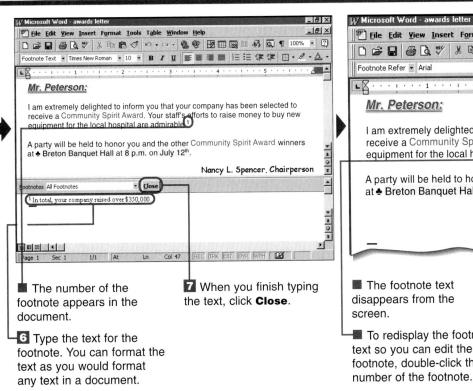

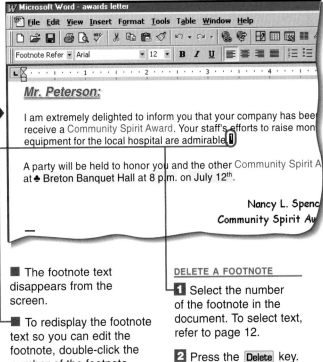

■ The number of the footnote appears in the document.

6 Type the text for the footnote. You can format the text as you would format any text in a document.

Note: To format text, refer to pages 92 to 109.

7 When you finish typing the text, click **Close**.

■ The footnote text disappears from the screen.

■ To redisplay the footnote text so you can edit the footnote, double-click the number of the footnote.

DELETE A FOOTNOTE

1 Select the number of the footnote in the document. To select text, refer to page 12.

2 Press the Delete key.

INSERT A PAGE BREAK

If you want to start a new page at a specific place in your document, you can insert a page break. A page break shows where one page ends and another begins.

INSERT A PAGE BREAK

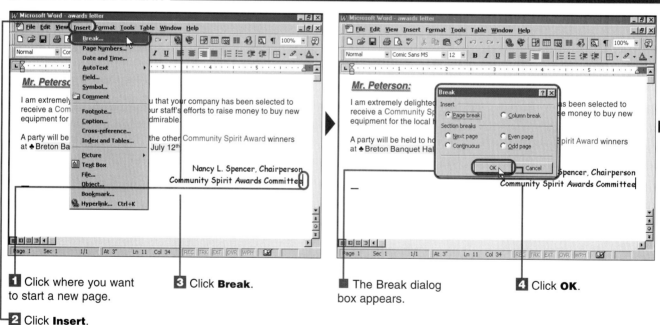

1 Click where you want to start a new page.

2 Click **Insert**.

3 Click **Break**.

■ The Break dialog box appears.

4 Click **OK**.

Will Word ever insert page breaks automatically?

When you fill a page with text, Word automatically starts a new page by inserting a page break for you.

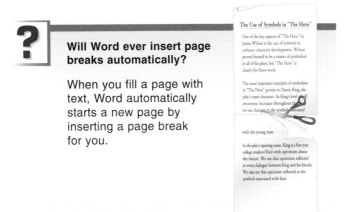

━ REMOVE A PAGE BREAK ━

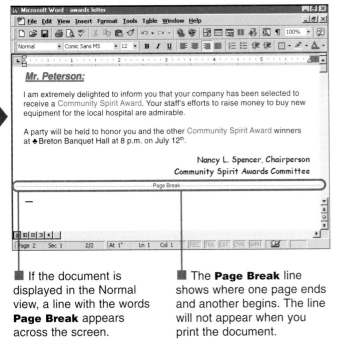

■ If the document is displayed in the Normal view, a line with the words **Page Break** appears across the screen.

■ The **Page Break** line shows where one page ends and another begins. The line will not appear when you print the document.

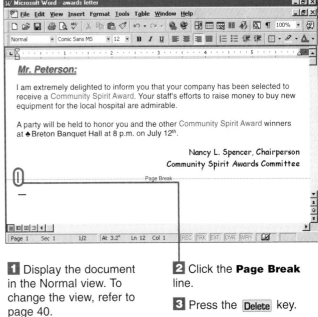

1 Display the document in the Normal view. To change the view, refer to page 40.

2 Click the **Page Break** line.

3 Press the Delete key.

INSERT A SECTION BREAK

You can divide your document into sections so you can format each section separately.

You need to divide a document into sections to change margins, create columns or vertically center text for only part of your document.

■ INSERT A SECTION BREAK

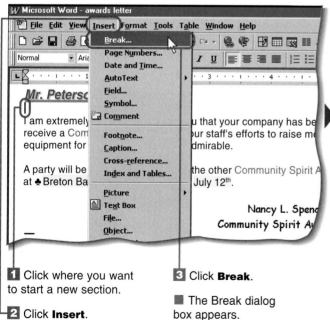

1 Click where you want to start a new section.

2 Click **Insert**.

3 Click **Break**.

■ The Break dialog box appears.

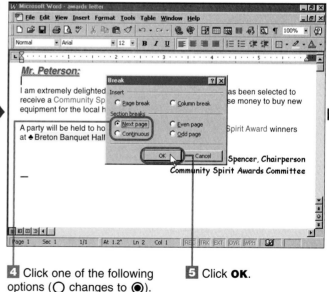

4 Click one of the following options (○ changes to ●).

Next page - Creates a new section on a new page.

Continuous - Creates a new section on the current page.

5 Click **OK**.

If I remove a section break will the appearance of my document change?

When you remove a section break, the text above the break assumes the appearance of the following section.

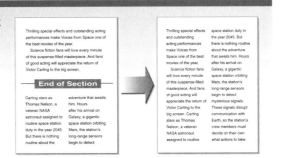

━ REMOVE A SECTION BREAK ━

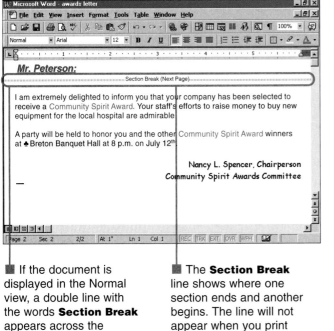

■ If the document is displayed in the Normal view, a double line with the words **Section Break** appears across the screen.

■ The **Section Break** line shows where one section ends and another begins. The line will not appear when you print the document.

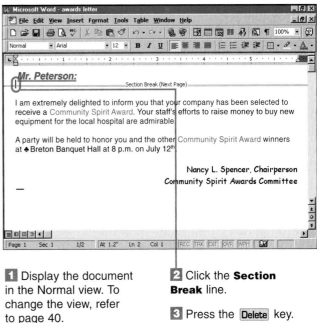

1 Display the document in the Normal view. To change the view, refer to page 40.

2 Click the **Section Break** line.

3 Press the Delete key.

CENTER TEXT ON A PAGE

You can vertically center
text on each page of a
document. This is useful
for creating title pages
or short memos.

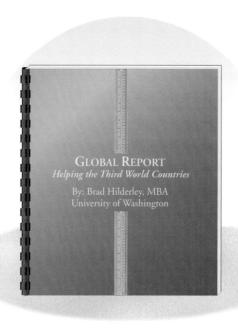

■ CENTER TEXT ON A PAGE ■

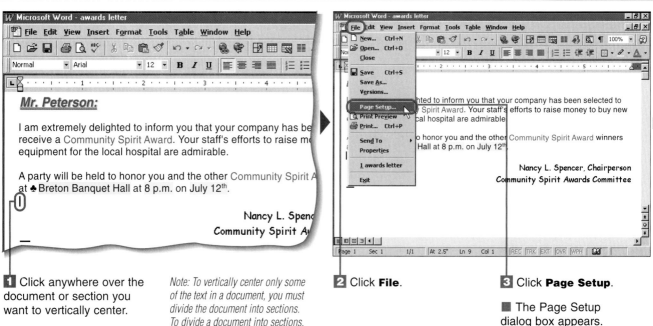

1 Click anywhere over the
document or section you
want to vertically center.

*Note: To vertically center only some
of the text in a document, you must
divide the document into sections.
To divide a document into sections,
refer to page 146.*

2 Click **File**.

3 Click **Page Setup**.

■ The Page Setup
dialog box appears.

148

?

How can I see what text centered on a page will look like when printed?

You can use the Print Preview feature to display a page on your screen. This lets you see how the page will look when printed.

Note: For information on using Print Preview, refer to page 176.

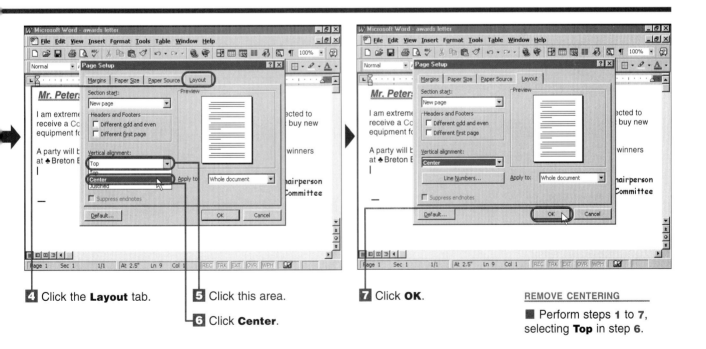

4 Click the **Layout** tab.

5 Click this area.

6 Click **Center**.

7 Click **OK**.

REMOVE CENTERING

■ Perform steps **1** to **7**, selecting **Top** in step **6**.

ADD A BORDER TO A PAGE

You can place a border around each page of a document. Word offers two types of page borders.

You can use a line border for certificates or report title pages. You can use a colorful art border to enhance invitations or newsletters.

■ ADD A BORDER TO A PAGE

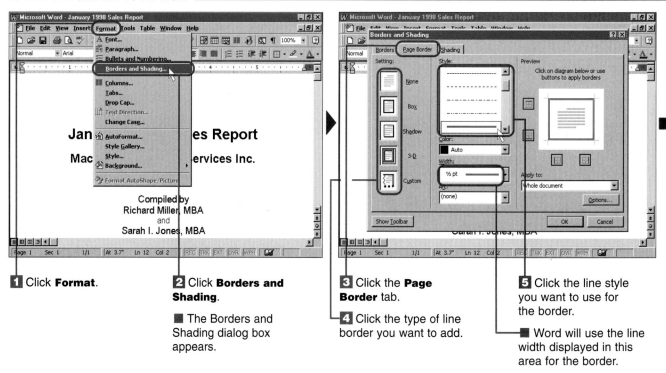

1 Click **Format**.

2 Click **Borders and Shading**.

■ The Borders and Shading dialog box appears.

3 Click the **Page Border** tab.

4 Click the type of line border you want to add.

5 Click the line style you want to use for the border.

■ Word will use the line width displayed in this area for the border.

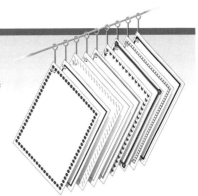

What styles of borders does Word offer?

These are some examples of the borders you can add to the pages in your document.

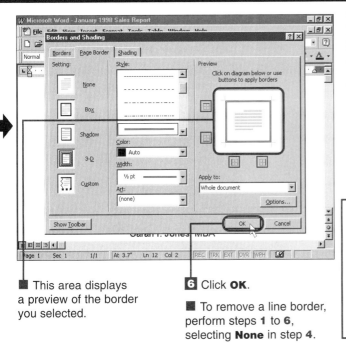

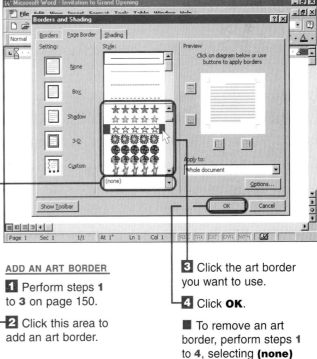

■ This area displays a preview of the border you selected.

6 Click **OK**.

■ To remove a line border, perform steps **1** to **6**, selecting **None** in step **4**.

ADD AN ART BORDER

1 Perform steps **1** to **3** on page 150.

2 Click this area to add an art border.

3 Click the art border you want to use.

4 Click **OK**.

■ To remove an art border, perform steps **1** to **4**, selecting **(none)** in step **3**.

CHANGE MARGINS

A margin is the amount of space between text and the edge of your paper. You can easily change the margins to suit your document.

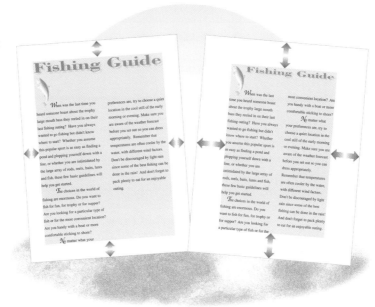

Changing margins lets you accommodate letterhead and other specialty paper.

CHANGE MARGINS

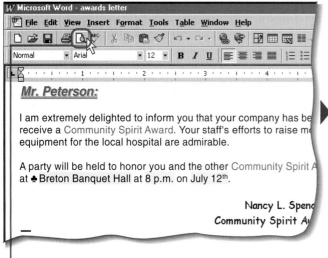

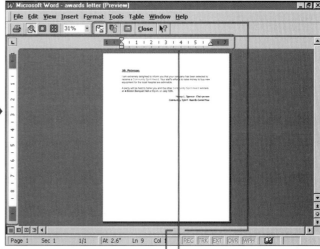

1 To change the margins for the entire document, click 🔍.

Note: To change the margins for only part of your document, refer to the top of page 153.

■ The document appears in the Print Preview window. For more information on using Print Preview, refer to page 176.

■ This area displays the ruler.

■ If the ruler is not displayed, click 📄.

How can I change the margins for only part of my document?

If you want to change the left and right margins for only part of your document, change the indentation of paragraphs. To indent paragraphs, refer to page 114.

If you want to change the top and bottom margins for only part of your document, you must divide the document into sections. To divide a document into sections, refer to page 146.

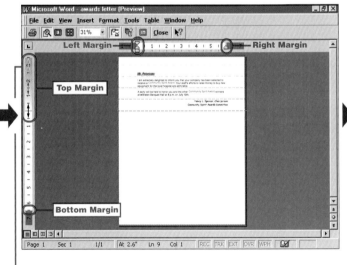

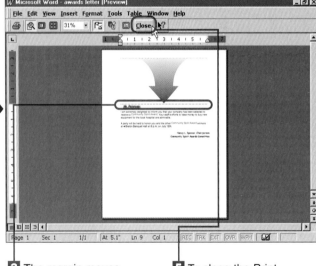

2 Click the margin you want to move (⬚ changes to ↕ or ↔) and then drag the margin to a new location.

■ A line shows the new location.

Note: To view the exact measurement of a margin, press and hold down the **Alt** *key as you perform step* **2**.

3 The margin moves to the new location.

4 Repeat steps **2** and **3** for each margin you want to move.

5 To close the Print Preview window, click **Close**.

CONTROL PAGE BREAKS

You can control the page breaks in a long document to tell Word how you want text to flow from one page to the next.

■ **CONTROL PAGE BREAKS** ■

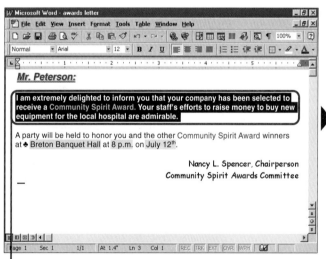

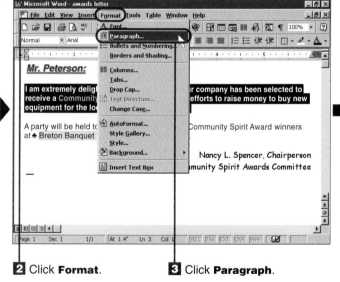

1 Select the paragraph(s) you want to control the page breaks for. To select text, refer to page 12.

2 Click **Format**.

3 Click **Paragraph**.

■ The Paragraph dialog box appears.

What are widows and orphans?

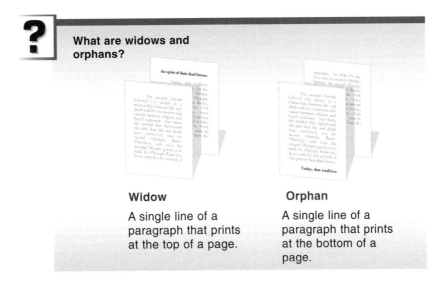

Widow

A single line of a paragraph that prints at the top of a page.

Orphan

A single line of a paragraph that prints at the bottom of a page.

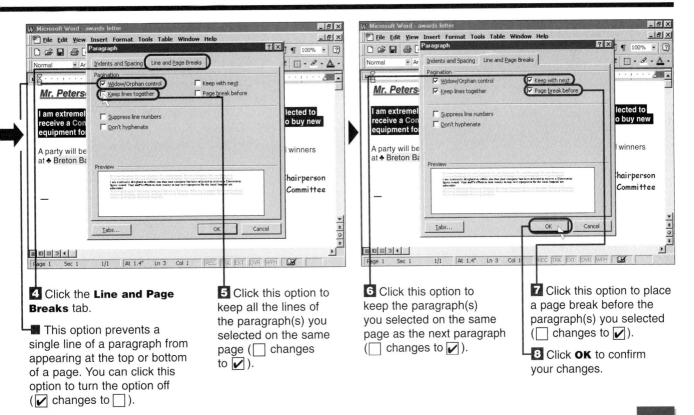

4 Click the **Line and Page Breaks** tab.

■ This option prevents a single line of a paragraph from appearing at the top or bottom of a page. You can click this option to turn the option off (✔ changes to ☐).

5 Click this option to keep all the lines of the paragraph(s) you selected on the same page (☐ changes to ✔).

6 Click this option to keep the paragraph(s) you selected on the same page as the next paragraph (☐ changes to ✔).

7 Click this option to place a page break before the paragraph(s) you selected (☐ changes to ✔).

8 Click **OK** to confirm your changes.

CHANGE PAPER SIZE

Word sets each page in your document to print on letter-sized paper. If you want to use a different paper size, you can change this setting.

■ CHANGE PAPER SIZE ■

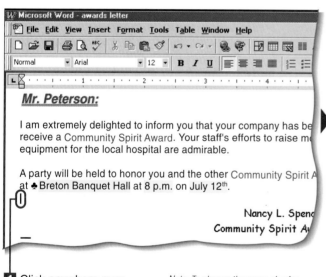

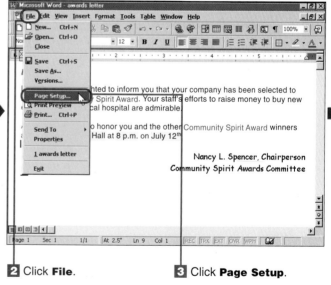

1 Click anywhere over the document or section you want to print on a different paper size.

Note: To change the paper size for only part of your document, you must divide the document into sections. To divide a document into sections, refer to page 146.

2 Click **File**.

3 Click **Page Setup**.

■ The Page Setup dialog box appears.

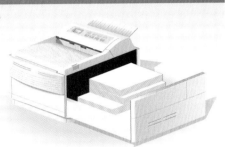

What paper sizes can I use?

The paper sizes listed in the Page Setup dialog box depend on the printer you are using.

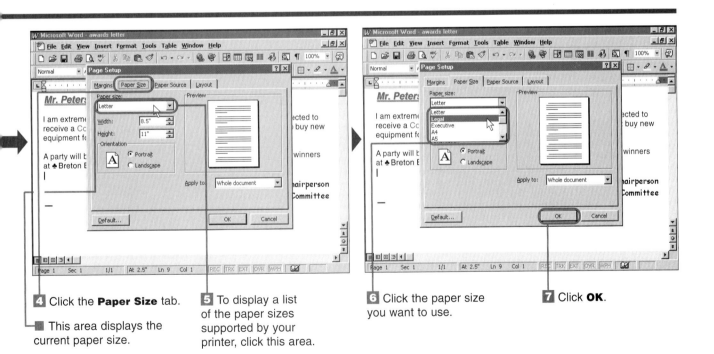

4 Click the **Paper Size** tab.

■ This area displays the current paper size.

5 To display a list of the paper sizes supported by your printer, click this area.

6 Click the paper size you want to use.

7 Click **OK**.

CHANGE PAGE ORIENTATION

You can change the orientation of pages in your document.

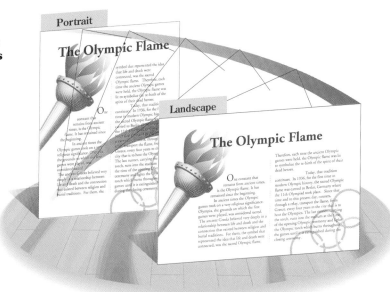

Portrait

Landscape

The Olympic Flame

CHANGE PAGE ORIENTATION

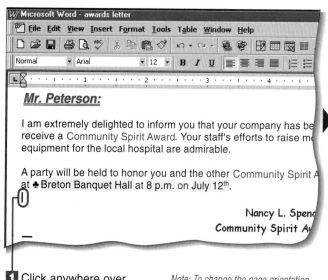

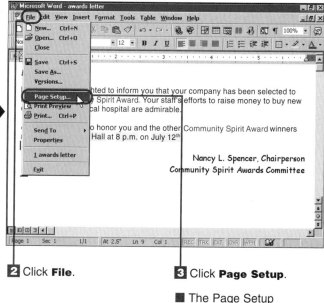

1 Click anywhere over the document or section you want to change to a different page orientation.

Note: To change the page orientation for only part of your document, you must divide the document into sections. To divide a document into sections, refer to page 146.

2 Click **File**.

3 Click **Page Setup**.

■ The Page Setup dialog box appears.

When would I use each page orientation?

Portrait

This is the standard page orientation. Most documents use the Portrait orientation.

Landscape

Certificates and tables often use the Landscape orientation.

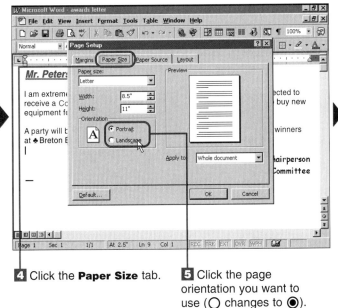

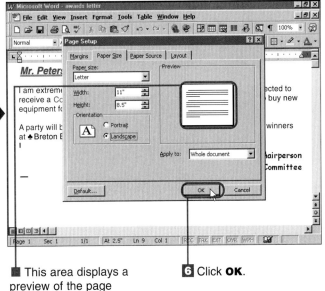

4 Click the **Paper Size** tab.

5 Click the page orientation you want to use (○ changes to ●).

■ This area displays a preview of the page orientation you selected.

6 Click **OK**.

CREATE NEWSPAPER COLUMNS

You can display your text in columns like those found in a newspaper. This is useful for creating documents such as newsletters and brochures.

■ CREATE NEWSPAPER COLUMNS

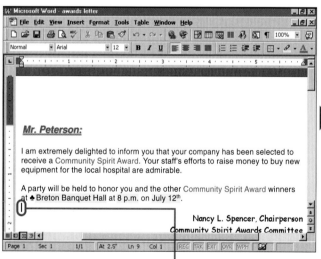

1 Display the document in the Page Layout view. To change the view, refer to page 40.

Note: Word does not display newspaper columns side-by-side in the Normal view.

2 Click anywhere over the document or section you want to display newspaper columns.

Note: To create newspaper columns for only part of the document, you must divide the document into sections. To divide a document into sections, refer to page 146.

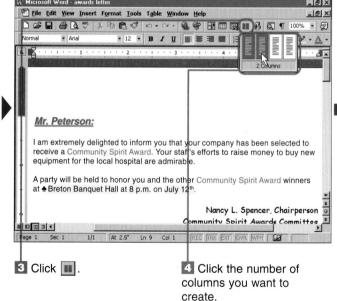

3 Click ▤.

4 Click the number of columns you want to create.

Why is there text in only one of my columns?

Word fills one column with text before starting a new column.

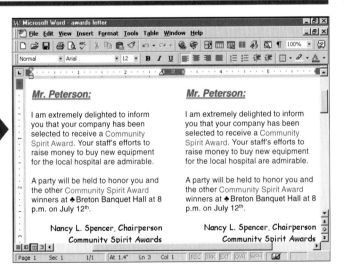

■ The text in the document appears in newspaper columns.

Note: For this example, the existing text was copied to show the newspaper columns. To copy text, refer to page 60.

■ REMOVE NEWSPAPER COLUMNS ■

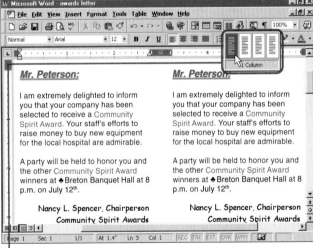

■ Repeat steps **2** to **4**, selecting **1 Column** in step **4**.

· Styles Museum

VOICES FROM SPACE

A Must See!!!
Thrilling special effects and outstanding acting performances make Voices from Space one of the best movies of the year.

The Plot
Victor Carling stars as Thomas Nelson, a veteran NASA astronaut aboard a gigantic space station orbiting Mars in the year 2045.

VOICES FROM SPACE

A MUST SEE!!!
Thrilling special effects and outstanding acting performances make Voices from Space one of the best movies of the year.

THE PLOT
Victor Carling stars as Thomas Nelson, a veteran NASA astronaut aboard a gigantic space station orbiting Mars in the year 2045.

CHAPTER 9

Smart Formatting

Would you like to format your documents automatically? Do you want to learn how to create, apply and change styles? This chapter teaches you how.

VOICES FROM SPACE

A Must See!!!

Thrilling special effects and outstanding acting performances make Voices from Space one of the best movies of the year.

The Plot

Victor Carling stars as Thomas Nelson, a veteran NASA astronaut aboard a gigantic space station orbiting Mars in the year 2045.

FORMAT A DOCUMENT AUTOMATICALLY

You can use the AutoFormat feature to instantly change a plain document with no formatting into a professional-looking document. Word will choose a design that best suits your document and then apply the design for you.

FORMAT A DOCUMENT AUTOMATICALLY

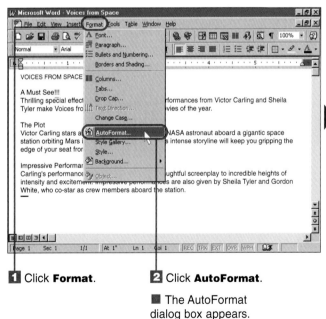

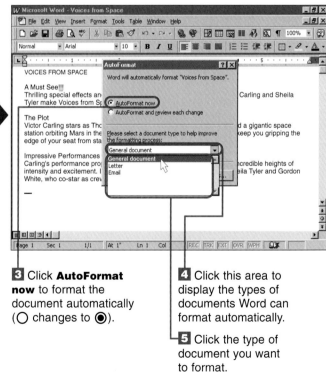

1 Click **Format**.

2 Click **AutoFormat**.

■ The AutoFormat dialog box appears.

3 Click **AutoFormat now** to format the document automatically (○ changes to ⦿).

4 Click this area to display the types of documents Word can format automatically.

5 Click the type of document you want to format.

Will the formatting changes affect my entire document?

When you format a document automatically, Word formats the entire document. However, if your document contains tables, the tables will not be affected by the new formats.

To automatically format a table, refer to page 214.

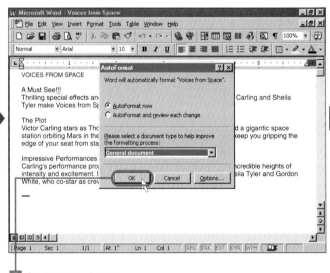

6 Click **OK** to format the document.

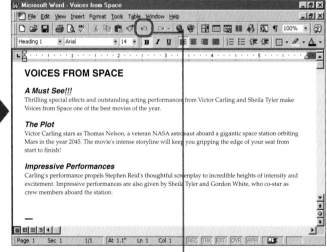

■ The document displays the new design.

■ If you do not like the new design, immediately click ☜ to remove the formatting.

USING THE STYLE GALLERY

After using the AutoFormat feature to format your document automatically, you can use the Style Gallery to quickly give your document a different look.

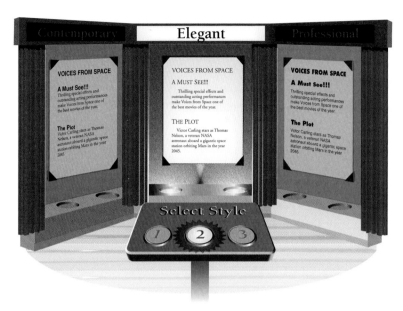

For information on formatting a document automatically, refer to page 164.

USING THE STYLE GALLERY

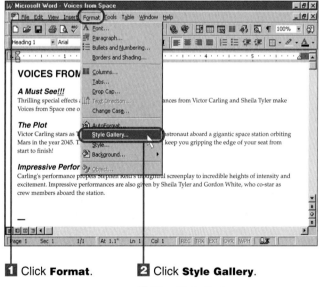

1 Click **Format**.

2 Click **Style Gallery**.

■ The Style Gallery dialog box appears.

■ This area displays the designs you can use to give your document a new look.

3 Click the design you want to use.

What types of designs does Word offer?

Word offers three types of designs in the Style Gallery.

Contemporary   Elegant   Professional

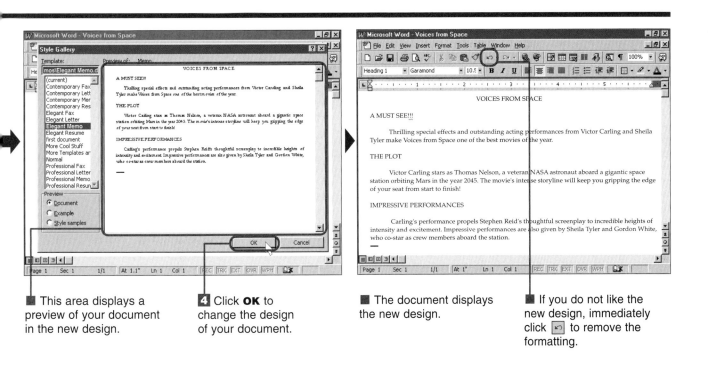

■ This area displays a preview of your document in the new design.

4 Click **OK** to change the design of your document.

■ The document displays the new design.

■ If you do not like the new design, immediately click 🖎 to remove the formatting.

CREATE A STYLE

Styles allow you to store formatting you like and apply the formatting to text in one step. You can easily create your own styles.

■ CREATE A STYLE

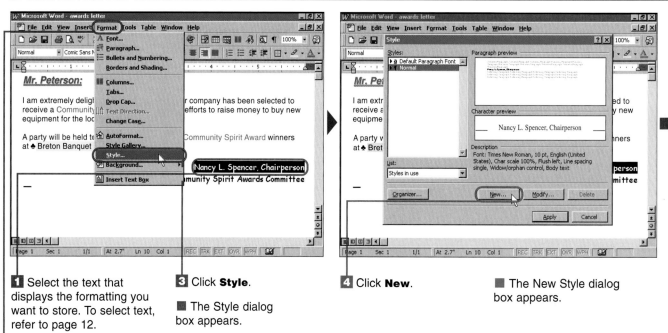

1 Select the text that displays the formatting you want to store. To select text, refer to page 12.

2 Click **Format**.

3 Click **Style**.

■ The Style dialog box appears.

4 Click **New**.

■ The New Style dialog box appears.

? What is the difference between paragraph and character styles?

Paragraph style

A paragraph style includes formatting that changes the appearance of individual characters and entire paragraphs, such as text alignment, tab settings and line spacing.

Character style

A character style includes formatting that changes the appearance of individual characters, such as **bold**, underline and text color.

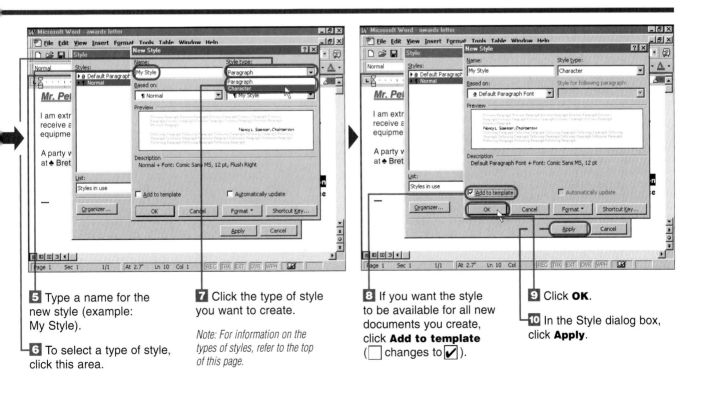

5 Type a name for the new style (example: My Style).

6 To select a type of style, click this area.

7 Click the type of style you want to create.

Note: For information on the types of styles, refer to the top of this page.

8 If you want the style to be available for all new documents you create, click **Add to template** (☐ changes to ☑).

9 Click **OK**.

10 In the Style dialog box, click **Apply**.

APPLY A STYLE

After you create a
style, you can apply
the style to text in
your document.

■ APPLY A STYLE

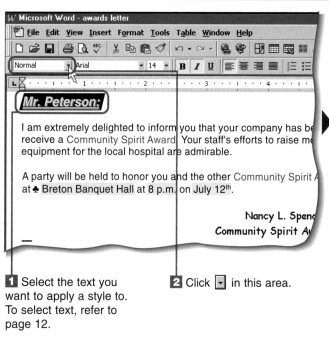

1 Select the text you
want to apply a style to.
To select text, refer to
page 12.

2 Click ▼ in this area.

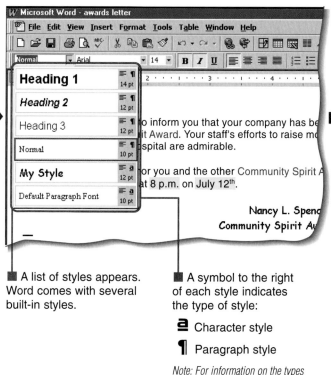

■ A list of styles appears.
Word comes with several
built-in styles.

■ A symbol to the right
of each style indicates
the type of style:

ª Character style

¶ Paragraph style

*Note: For information on the types
of styles, refer to the top of page 169.*

How can using styles help me?

Styles can save you time when you want to apply the same formatting to many different areas in a document. Styles also help you keep the appearance of text in a document consistent.

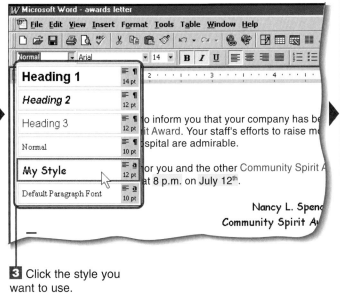

3 Click the style you want to use.

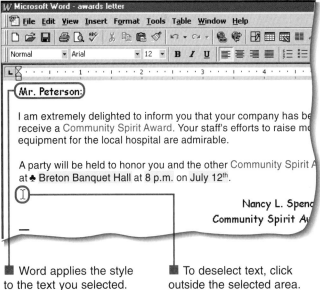

■ Word applies the style to the text you selected.

■ To deselect text, click outside the selected area.

CHANGE A STYLE

You can easily make changes to a style you created. All text formatted using the style will automatically display the changes.

■ CHANGE A STYLE ■

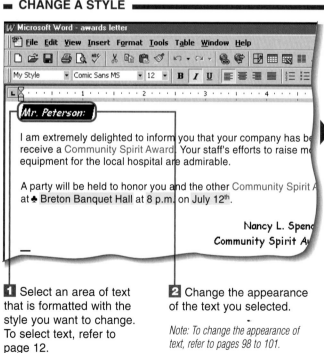

1 Select an area of text that is formatted with the style you want to change. To select text, refer to page 12.

2 Change the appearance of the text you selected.

Note: To change the appearance of text, refer to pages 98 to 101.

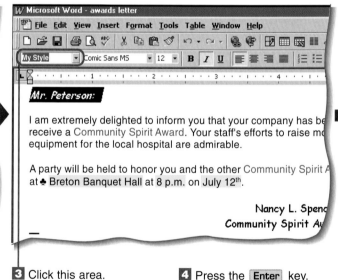

3 Click this area.

4 Press the **Enter** key.

When would I want to change a style?

You may want to change an existing style to quickly change the appearance of a document. You can try several formats until the document appears the way you want.

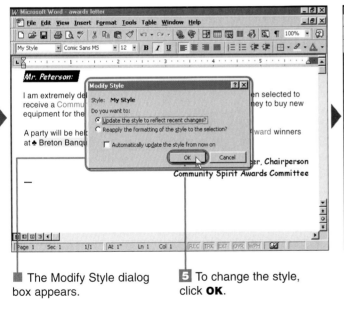

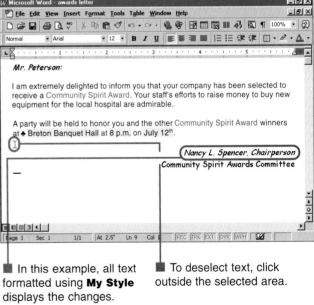

■ The Modify Style dialog box appears.

5 To change the style, click **OK**.

■ In this example, all text formatted using **My Style** displays the changes.

■ To deselect text, click outside the selected area.

CHAPTER 10

Print Your Documents

Now that I have created my document, how do I produce a paper copy? Find out how to print your documents, envelopes and labels in this chapter.

PREVIEW A DOCUMENT

You can use the Print Preview feature to see how your document will look when printed.

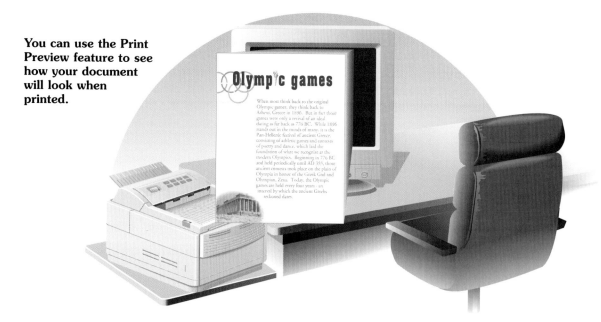

■ PREVIEW A DOCUMENT

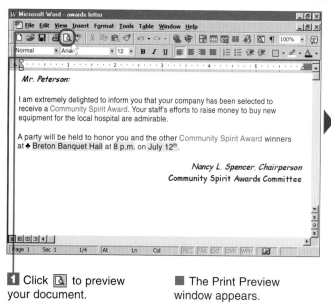

1 Click 🔍 to preview your document.

■ The Print Preview window appears.

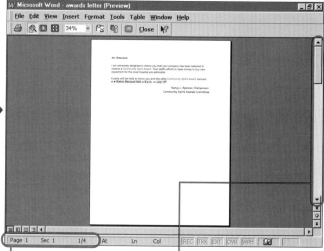

■ This area tells you which page is displayed and the number of pages in the document. In this example, the document contains four pages.

■ If your document contains more than one page, use the scroll bar to view the other pages. To use the scroll bar, refer to page 15.

When can I edit my document in the Print Preview window?

*Note: To change the shape of the mouse, perform step **2** below.*

If the mouse looks like I when over your document, you can edit the document.

If the mouse looks like ⊕ or ⊖ when over your document, you can magnify or shrink the page displayed on the screen.

MAGNIFY A PAGE

1 Position the mouse over the page (⬚ changes to ⊕).

2 If the mouse looks like I (not ⊕) when over the page, click 🔍.

3 Click the page to magnify the page.

■ A magnified view of the page appears.

■ To browse through the document, use the scroll bar.

CONTINUED

PREVIEW A DOCUMENT

Word can display
several pages at once
in the Print Preview
window. This lets you
view the overall style
of a long document.

PREVIEW A DOCUMENT (CONTINUED)

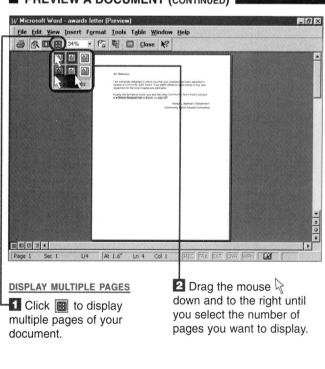

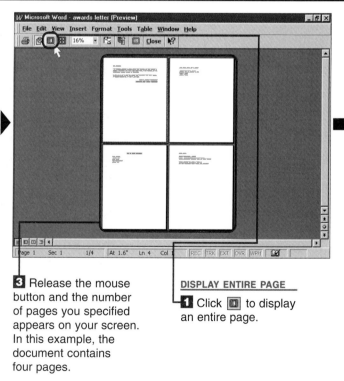

DISPLAY MULTIPLE PAGES

1 Click 🔲 to display
multiple pages of your
document.

2 Drag the mouse
down and to the right until
you select the number of
pages you want to display.

3 Release the mouse
button and the number
of pages you specified
appears on your screen.
In this example, the
document contains
four pages.

DISPLAY ENTIRE PAGE

1 Click 🔲 to display
an entire page.

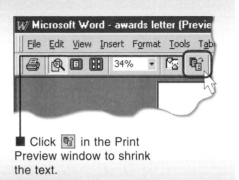

?

Can I shrink the text in my document to fit on fewer pages?

If the last page in your document contains only a few lines of text, Word can shrink the text to fit on one less page.

■ Click 🔁 in the Print Preview window to shrink the text.

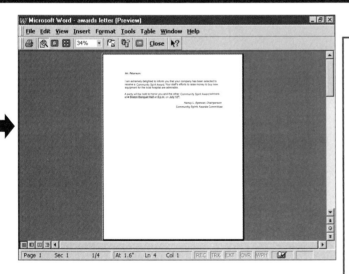

■ An entire page appears on your screen.

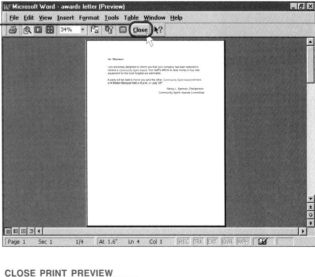

CLOSE PRINT PREVIEW

1 Click **Close** to close the Print Preview window.

PRINT A DOCUMENT

You can produce
a paper copy of the
document displayed
on your screen.

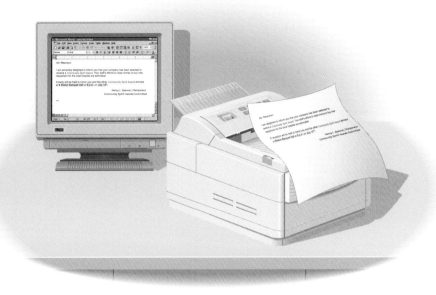

PRINT A DOCUMENT

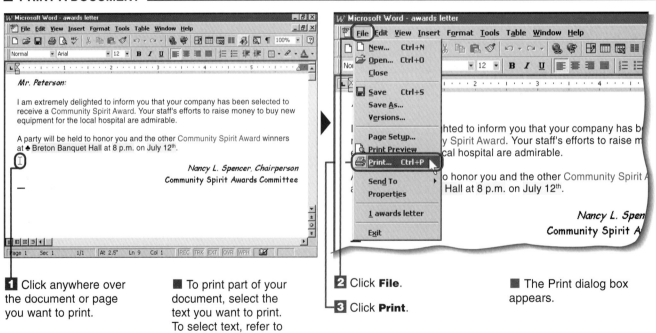

■ **1** Click anywhere over
the document or page
you want to print.

■ To print part of your
document, select the
text you want to print.
To select text, refer to
page 12.

■ **2** Click **File**.

■ **3** Click **Print**.

■ The Print dialog box
appears.

How do I prepare my printer to print documents?

Before printing, always make sure your printer is turned on and contains paper.

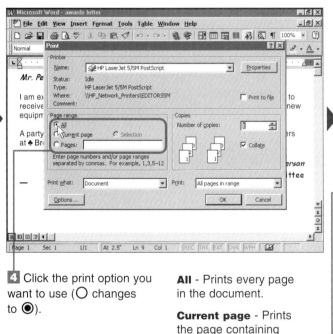

4 Click the print option you want to use (○ changes to ◉).

All - Prints every page in the document.

Current page - Prints the page containing the insertion point.

Pages - Prints the pages you specify.

Selection - Prints the text you selected.

■ If you selected **Pages** in step **4**, type the pages you want to print (example: 1,3,5 or 2-4).

5 Click **OK**.

QUICKLY PRINT ENTIRE DOCUMENT

1 To quickly print an entire document, click 🖨 .

PRINT AN ENVELOPE

You can easily
print an address
on an envelope.

■ PRINT AN ENVELOPE

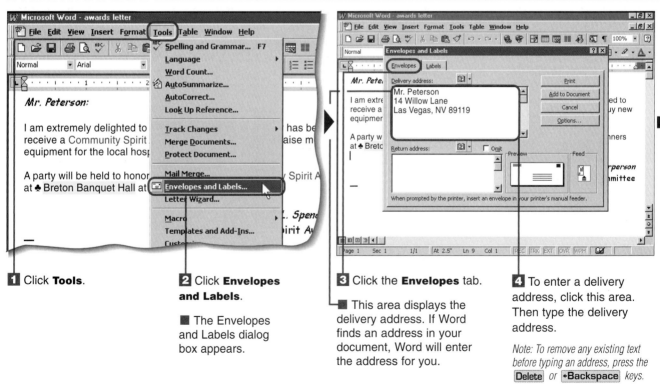

1 Click **Tools**.

2 Click **Envelopes and Labels**.

■ The Envelopes and Labels dialog box appears.

3 Click the **Envelopes** tab.

■ This area displays the delivery address. If Word finds an address in your document, Word will enter the address for you.

4 To enter a delivery address, click this area. Then type the delivery address.

Note: To remove any existing text before typing an address, press the **Delete** *or* **+Backspace** *keys.*

? Why would I omit the return address on an envelope?

You would omit the return address if your envelope already displays a return address. Company stationery often displays a return address.

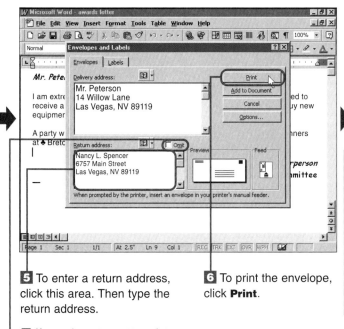

5 To enter a return address, click this area. Then type the return address.

■ If you do not want to print a return address, click **Omit**.

6 To print the envelope, click **Print**.

■ This dialog box appears if you entered a return address.

7 To save the return address, click **Yes**.

*Note: If you selected **Yes** in step 7, the address will appear as the return address every time you print an envelope. This saves you from constantly having to retype the address.*

PRINT LABELS

Word helps you print labels.

PRINT LABELS

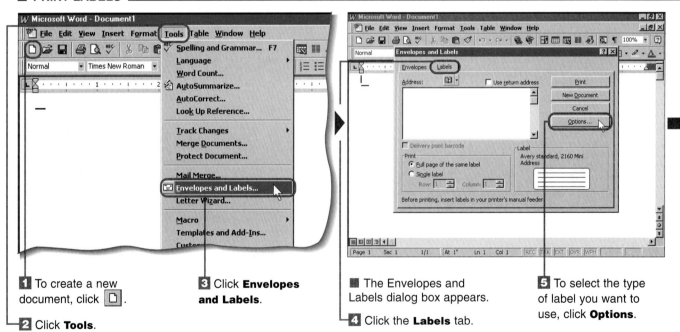

1 To create a new document, click 🗋.

2 Click **Tools**.

3 Click **Envelopes and Labels**.

■ The Envelopes and Labels dialog box appears.

4 Click the **Labels** tab.

5 To select the type of label you want to use, click **Options**.

How can I tell which label product I am using?

You can check your label packaging to determine which label product to select in step **7** below.

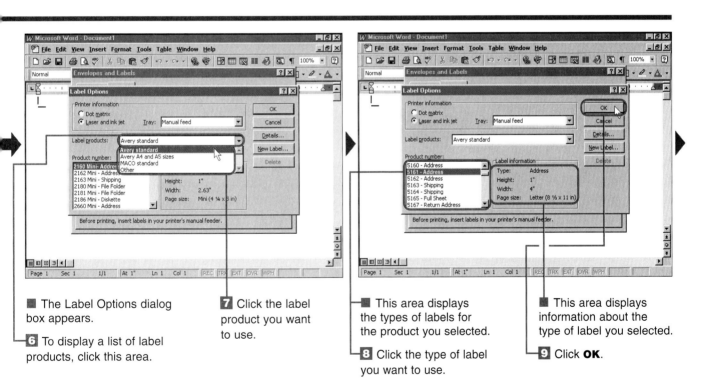

■ The Label Options dialog box appears.

6 To display a list of label products, click this area.

7 Click the label product you want to use.

■ This area displays the types of labels for the product you selected.

8 Click the type of label you want to use.

■ This area displays information about the type of label you selected.

9 Click **OK**.

CONTINUED

PRINT LABELS

You can use labels for
envelopes, file folders,
diskettes, video cassettes
and name tags.

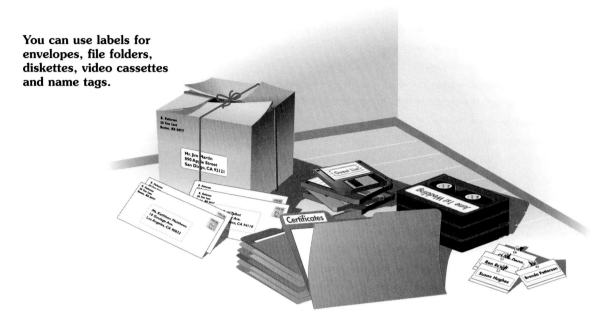

■ PRINT LABELS (CONTINUED)

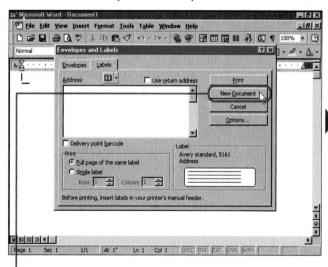

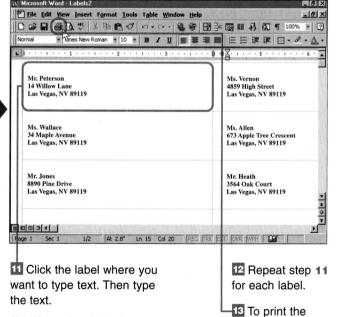

10 To add the labels
to a new document,
click **New Document**.

■ The labels appear.

11 Click the label where you
want to type text. Then type
the text.

*Note: You can format the text as you
would format any text in a document.
To format text, refer to pages 92 to 109.*

12 Repeat step **11**
for each label.

13 To print the
labels, click 🖨.

?

Can I quickly create a label for each person on my mailing list?

You can use the Mail Merge feature included with Word to quickly create a label for each person on your mailing list. For more information, refer to page 270.

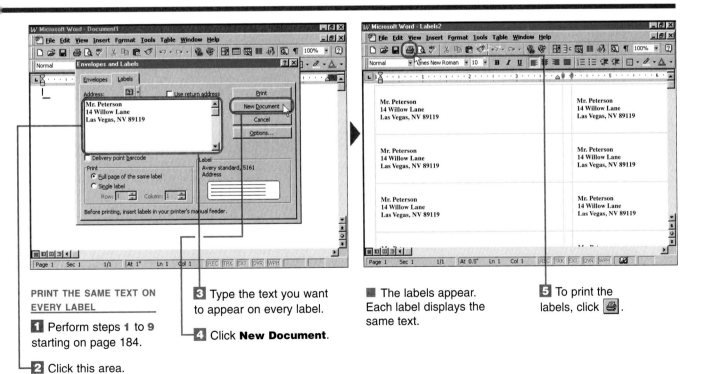

PRINT THE SAME TEXT ON EVERY LABEL

1 Perform steps **1** to **9** starting on page 184.

2 Click this area.

3 Type the text you want to appear on every label.

4 Click **New Document**.

■ The labels appear. Each label displays the same text.

5 To print the labels, click 🖨.

CHANGE PAPER SOURCE

You can change the
location where Word
will look for the paper
to print your document.

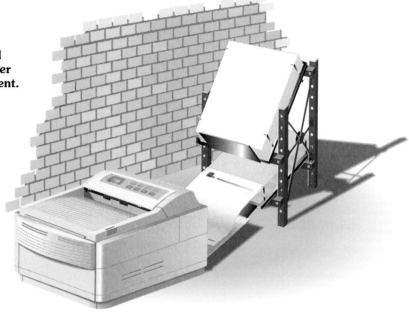

■ CHANGE PAPER SOURCE

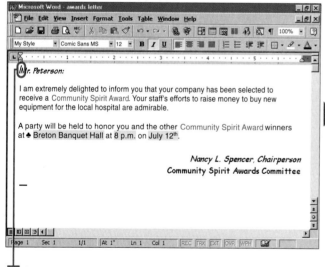

1 Click anywhere over
the document or section
you want to print on
different paper.

*Note: To change the paper source
for only part of your document,
you must divide the document into
sections. To divide a document
into sections, refer to page 146.*

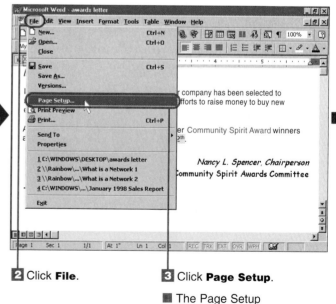

2 Click **File**.

3 Click **Page Setup**.

■ The Page Setup
dialog box appears.

? **Why would I change the paper source?**

Changing the paper source is useful if your printer stores letterhead in one location and plain paper in another location. You can print the first page of your document on letterhead and print the rest of the document on plain paper.

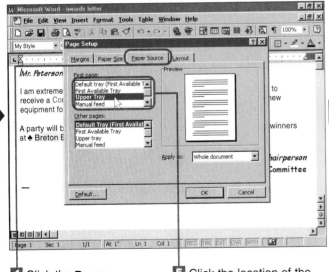

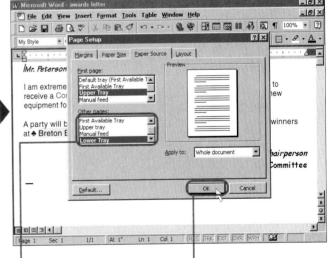

4 Click the **Paper Source** tab.

5 Click the location of the paper you want to use for the first page of your document in this area.

Note: The options available in this area depend on your printer.

6 Click the location of the paper you want to use for the other pages of your document in this area.

Note: The options available in this area depend on your printer.

7 Click **OK**.

CHAPTER 11

Work with Multiple Documents

Wondering how to create new documents and work with more than one document? Learn how in this chapter.

CREATE A NEW DOCUMENT

You can create a new
document to start
writing a letter,
report or memo.

CREATE A NEW DOCUMENT

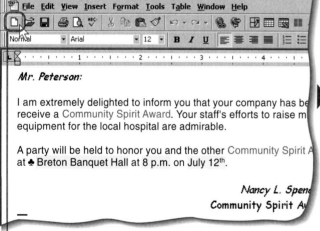

1 Click 🗋.

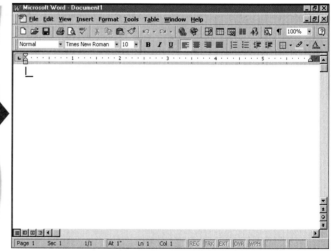

■ A new document appears.
The previous document is
now hidden behind the new
document.

■ Think of each document
as a separate piece of
paper. When you create a
document, you are placing
a new piece of paper on
the screen.

SWITCH BETWEEN DOCUMENTS

Word lets you have many documents open at once. You can easily switch from one open document to another.

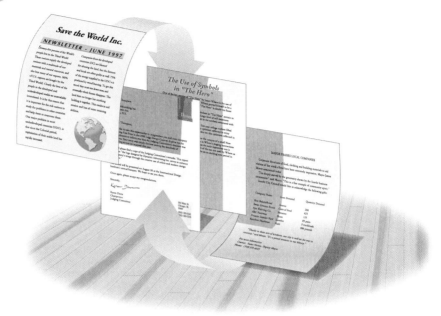

■ SWITCH BETWEEN DOCUMENTS

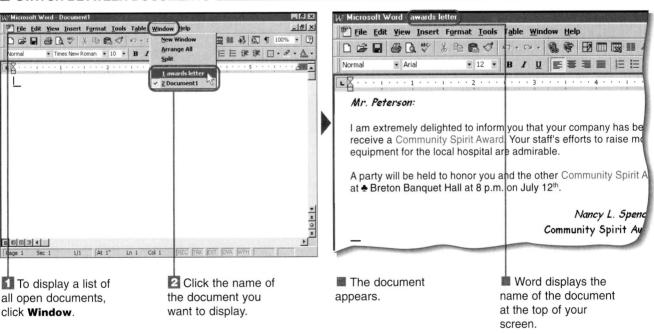

1 To display a list of all open documents, click **Window**.

2 Click the name of the document you want to display.

■ The document appears.

■ Word displays the name of the document at the top of your screen.

ARRANGE OPEN DOCUMENTS

If you have several documents
open, some of them may be
hidden. You can easily display
the contents of all your open
documents.

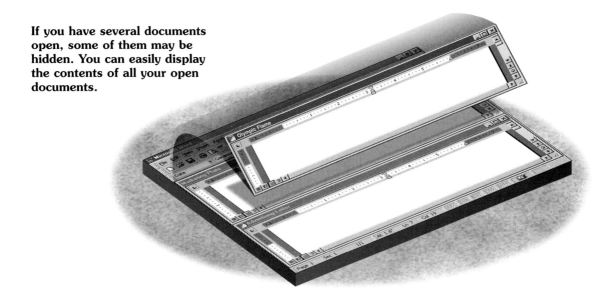

■ ARRANGE OPEN DOCUMENTS

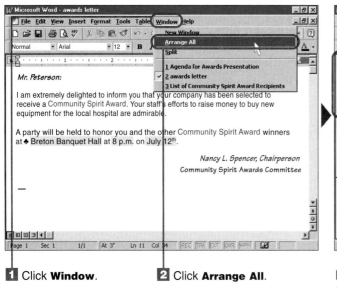

1 Click **Window**.

2 Click **Arrange All**.

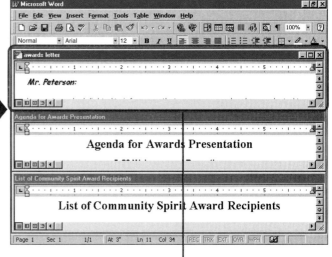

■ You can now view the
contents of all your open
documents.

■ You can only work in the
current document, which
displays a highlighted title
bar.

*Note: To make another document
current, click anywhere over the
document.*

You can enlarge a document to fill your screen. This lets you view more of its contents.

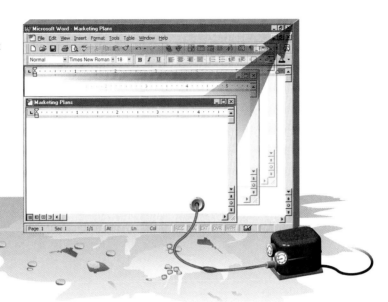

MAXIMIZE A DOCUMENT

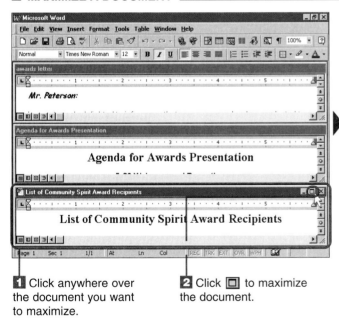

1 Click anywhere over the document you want to maximize.

2 Click 🔲 to maximize the document.

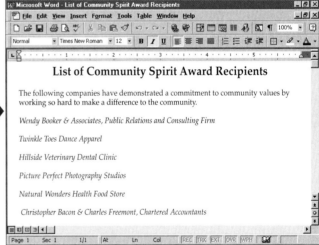

■ The document fills your screen.

Note: The maximized document covers all your open documents.

COPY OR MOVE TEXT BETWEEN DOCUMENTS

You can copy or move text from one document to another. This will save you time when you want to use text from another document.

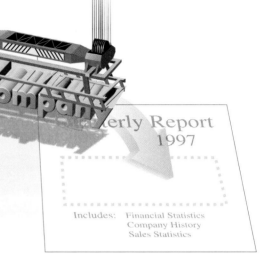

■ COPY OR MOVE TEXT BETWEEN DOCUMENTS ■

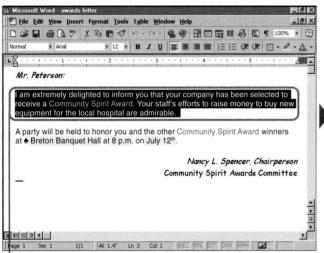

1 Select the text you want to place in another document. To select text, refer to page 12.

2 Click one of the following options:

⌗ Move the text

📋 Copy the text

Note: For information on the difference between moving and copying text, refer to the top of page 197.

?

What is the difference between moving and copying text?

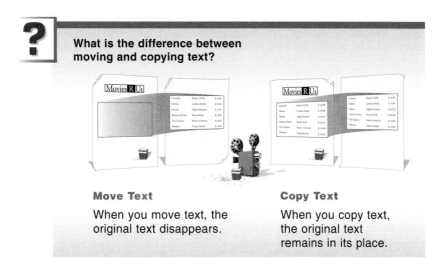

Move Text

When you move text, the original text disappears.

Copy Text

When you copy text, the original text remains in its place.

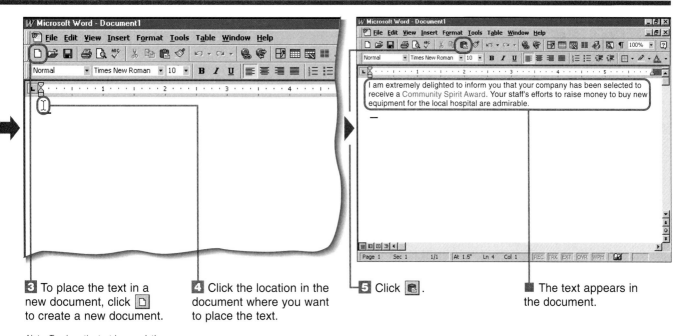

3 To place the text in a new document, click □ to create a new document.

Note: To place the text in an existing document, open the document. To open a document, refer to page 30.

4 Click the location in the document where you want to place the text.

5 Click 🖺.

■ The text appears in the document.

	Jan	Feb	Mar	Total
		7	5	19
East	7	7	7	
West	6	4	9	24
South	8	7	21	60
Total	21	18		

	Jan	Feb	Mar	Total
				19
East	7		7	17
West			9	24
South			21	60
Total		18		

ERASER

Company Name	Item Donated	Quantity Donated
Best Bakery	Bread	200 loaves
Swan Grocery Stores	Cans of food	425
Ajax Knitting Co.	Sweater	125
ABC Footwear	Shoes	85 pairs
Premier Lumber Yard	Lumber	5 truckloads
Rainbow Hardware	Nails	900 pounds

CHAPTER 12

Work with Tables

Do you want to learn how to display information in a table? This chapter teaches you how to create and work with a table in your document.

CREATE A TABLE

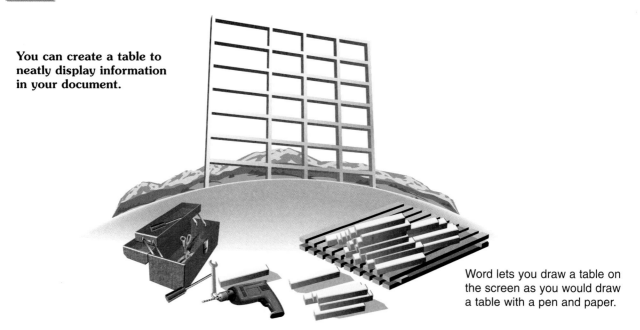

You can create a table to neatly display information in your document.

Word lets you draw a table on the screen as you would draw a table with a pen and paper.

■ CREATE A TABLE

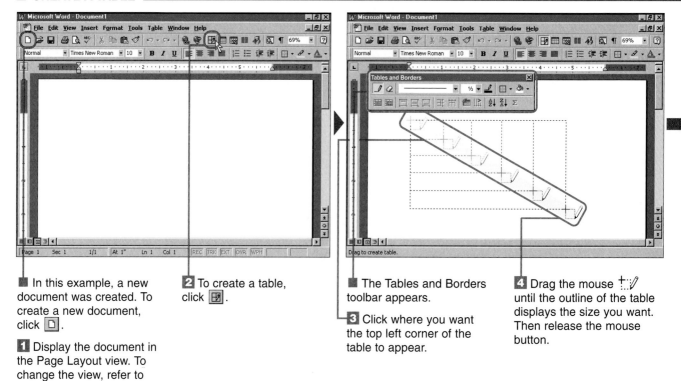

■ In this example, a new document was created. To create a new document, click 🗋.

1 Display the document in the Page Layout view. To change the view, refer to page 40.

2 To create a table, click 🎛.

■ The Tables and Borders toolbar appears.

3 Click where you want the top left corner of the table to appear.

4 Drag the mouse ✛ until the outline of the table displays the size you want. Then release the mouse button.

Can I move a toolbar out of the way?

If a toolbar is in the way, you can easily move the toolbar to a new location.

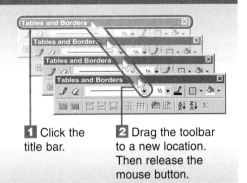

1 Click the title bar.

2 Drag the toolbar to a new location. Then release the mouse button.

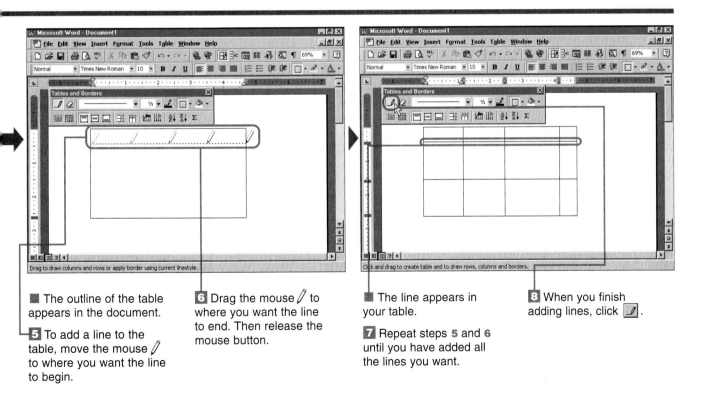

■ The outline of the table appears in the document.

5 To add a line to the table, move the mouse ∅ to where you want the line to begin.

6 Drag the mouse ∅ to where you want the line to end. Then release the mouse button.

■ The line appears in your table.

7 Repeat steps **5** and **6** until you have added all the lines you want.

8 When you finish adding lines, click ∅.

CHANGE ROW HEIGHT OR COLUMN WIDTH

After you have created
a table, you can change
the height of rows or
the width of columns.

■ CHANGE ROW HEIGHT

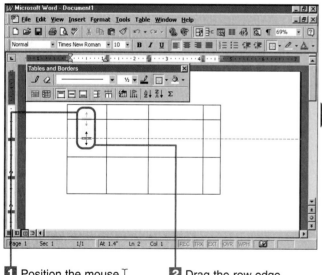

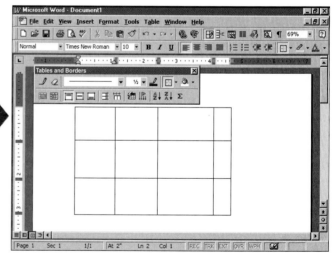

1 Position the mouse I
over the bottom edge
of the row you want to
change (I changes
to ＋).

2 Drag the row edge
to a new position.

■ A line shows the new
position.

3 Release the left
mouse button and
the row displays
the new height.

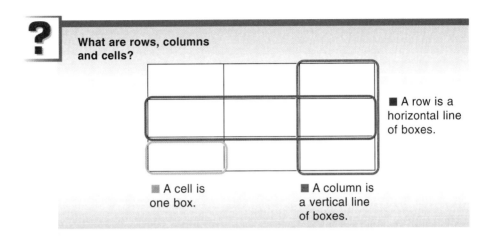

What are rows, columns and cells?

■ A row is a horizontal line of boxes.

■ A cell is one box.

■ A column is a vertical line of boxes.

■ CHANGE COLUMN WIDTH

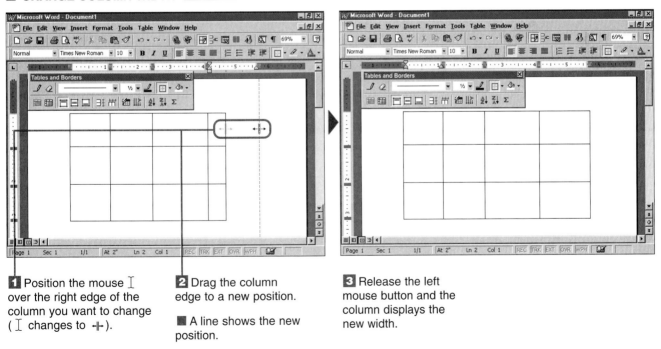

1 Position the mouse I over the right edge of the column you want to change (I changes to ↔).

2 Drag the column edge to a new position.

■ A line shows the new position.

3 Release the left mouse button and the column displays the new width.

ERASE LINES

You can easily erase lines from your table.

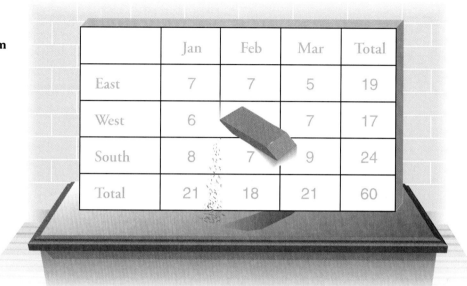

ERASE LINES

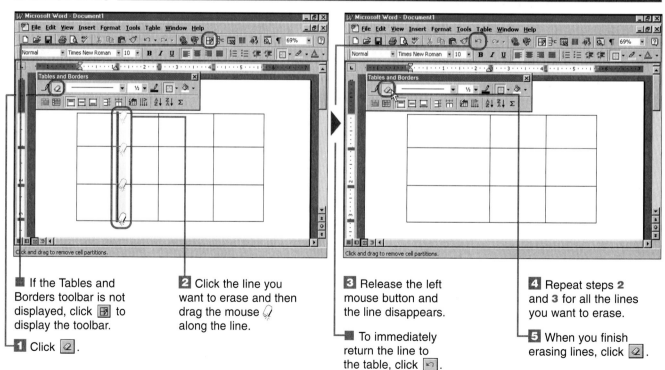

■ If the Tables and Borders toolbar is not displayed, click 🖽 to display the toolbar.

1 Click 🖉.

2 Click the line you want to erase and then drag the mouse 🖉 along the line.

3 Release the left mouse button and the line disappears.

■ To immediately return the line to the table, click 🖍.

4 Repeat steps **2** and **3** for all the lines you want to erase.

5 When you finish erasing lines, click 🖉.

You can easily enter text into the cells of a table.

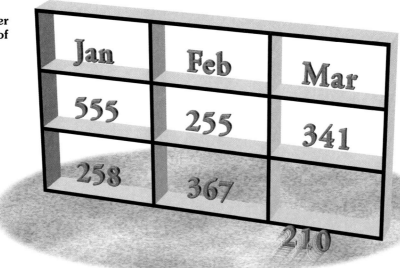

ENTER TEXT

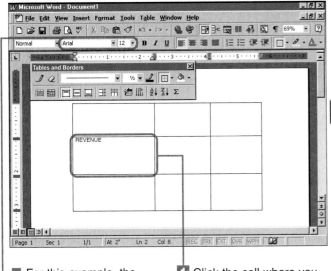

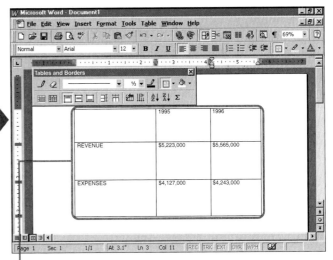

■ For this example, the design and size of text were changed to make the text easier to read. To change the design and size of text, refer to pages 94 and 95.

1 Click the cell where you want to type text. Then type the text.

Note: To quickly move through the cells in a table, press the ←, ↑, ↓ or → keys.

2 Repeat step 1 until you have typed all the text.

■ You can edit and format the text in a table as you would edit and format any text in a document.

ADD A ROW OR COLUMN

You can add a row or column to your table if you want to insert additional information.

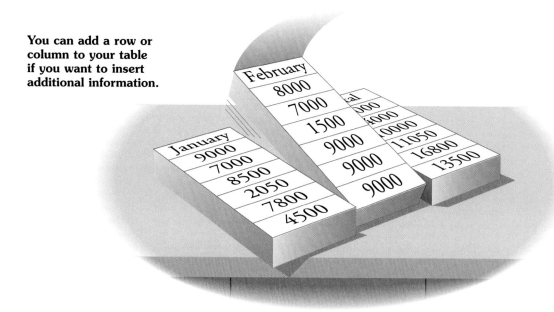

ADD A ROW

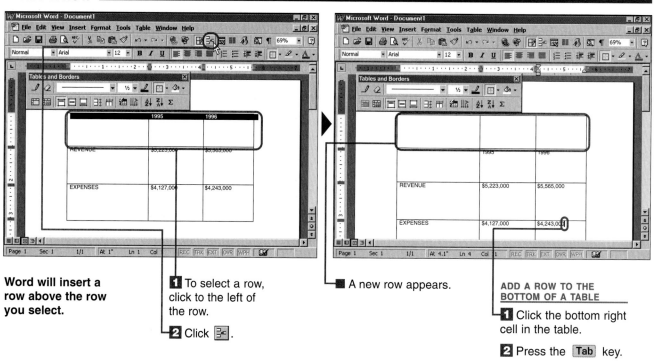

Word will insert a row above the row you select.

1 To select a row, click to the left of the row.

2 Click ⋺.

■ A new row appears.

ADD A ROW TO THE BOTTOM OF A TABLE

1 Click the bottom right cell in the table.

2 Press the **Tab** key.

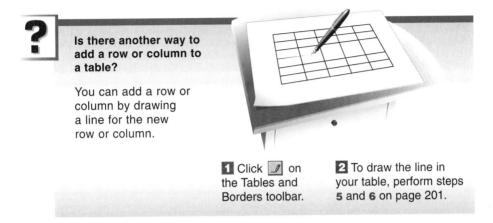

Is there another way to add a row or column to a table?

You can add a row or column by drawing a line for the new row or column.

1 Click 🖉 on the Tables and Borders toolbar.

2 To draw the line in your table, perform steps **5** and **6** on page 201.

■ ADD A COLUMN

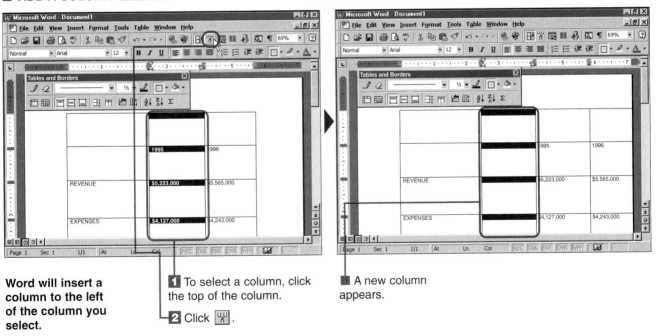

Word will insert a column to the left of the column you select.

1 To select a column, click the top of the column.

2 Click 🔠.

■ A new column appears.

DELETE A ROW OR COLUMN

You can delete a row or column you no longer need.

■ DELETE A ROW OR COLUMN

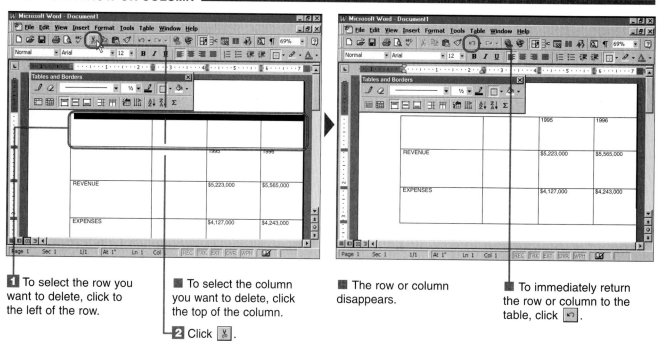

1 To select the row you want to delete, click to the left of the row.

■ To select the column you want to delete, click the top of the column.

2 Click ✂.

■ The row or column disappears.

■ To immediately return the row or column to the table, click ↩.

DELETE A TABLE

You can quickly remove
an entire table from your
document.

DELETE A TABLE

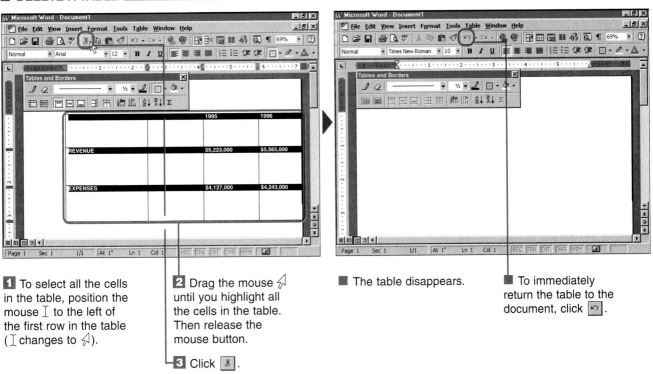

1 To select all the cells
in the table, position the
mouse I to the left of
the first row in the table
(I changes to ⇗).

2 Drag the mouse ⇗
until you highlight all
the cells in the table.
Then release the
mouse button.

3 Click ✂.

■ The table disappears.

■ To immediately
return the table to the
document, click ↶.

ALIGN TEXT IN CELLS

You can align text
at the top, center
or bottom of a cell
in your table.

ALIGN TEXT IN CELLS

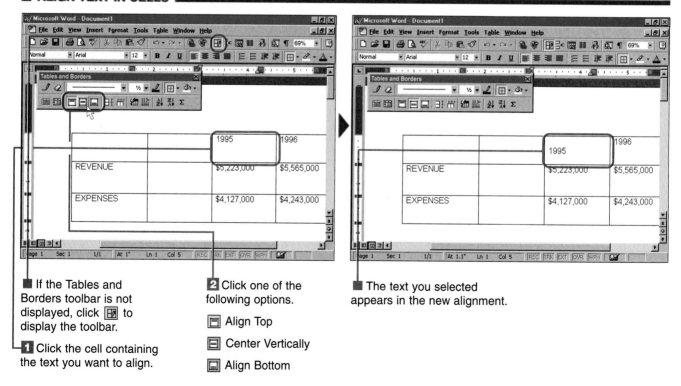

■ If the Tables and
Borders toolbar is not
displayed, click 🔲 to
display the toolbar.

1 Click the cell containing
the text you want to align.

2 Click one of the
following options.

🔳 Align Top

🔳 Center Vertically

🔳 Align Bottom

■ The text you selected
appears in the new alignment.

You can change the direction
of text in a cell. A different
direction can help emphasize
row and column headings in
your table.

■ CHANGE TEXT DIRECTION ■

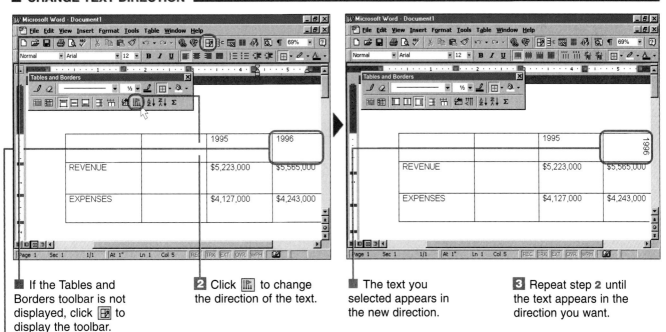

■ If the Tables and
Borders toolbar is not
displayed, click 🔳 to
display the toolbar.

■ Click the cell containing
the text you want to change.

2 Click 🔳 to change
the direction of the text.

■ The text you
selected appears in
the new direction.

3 Repeat step **2** until
the text appears in the
direction you want.

CHANGE TABLE BORDERS

You can enhance the
appearance of a table by
changing the borders.

■ CHANGE TABLE BORDERS

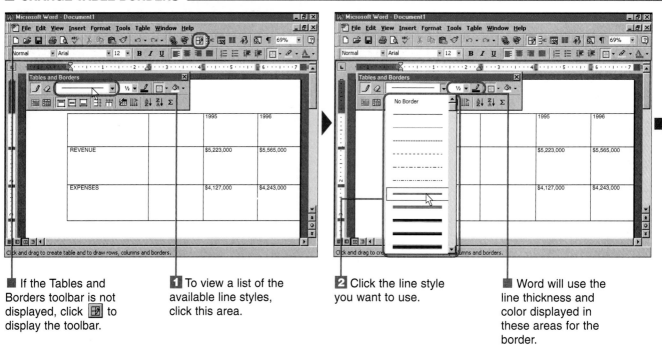

■ If the Tables and
Borders toolbar is not
displayed, click 🔲 to
display the toolbar.

1 To view a list of the
available line styles,
click this area.

2 Click the line style
you want to use.

■ Word will use the
line thickness and
color displayed in
these areas for the
border.

How can I quickly enhance the appearance of a table?

Company Name	Item Dona...d	Quantity Donated
Best Bakery	Bread	200 loaves
Swan Grocery Stores	Cans of ...od	425
Ajax Knitting Co.	Sweate...	125
ABC Footwear	Shoes	85 pairs
Premier Lumber Yard	Lumb...	5 truckloads
Rainbow Hardware	Nails	900 pounds

You can have Word automatically add borders and shading to a table by using the Table AutoFormat feature. For information on the Table AutoFormat feature, refer to page 214.

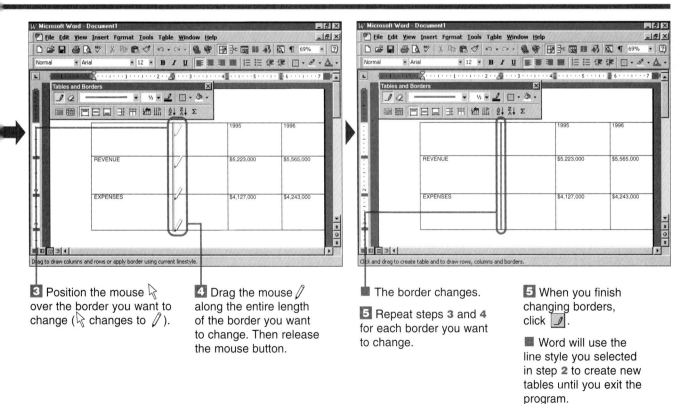

3 Position the mouse ⬉ over the border you want to change (⬉ changes to ⫽).

4 Drag the mouse ⫽ along the entire length of the border you want to change. Then release the mouse button.

◼ The border changes.

5 Repeat steps **3** and **4** for each border you want to change.

5 When you finish changing borders, click 🖉.

◼ Word will use the line style you selected in step **2** to create new tables until you exit the program.

FORMAT A TABLE

Word offers many ready-to-use designs that you can choose from to give your table a new appearance.

■ FORMAT A TABLE ■

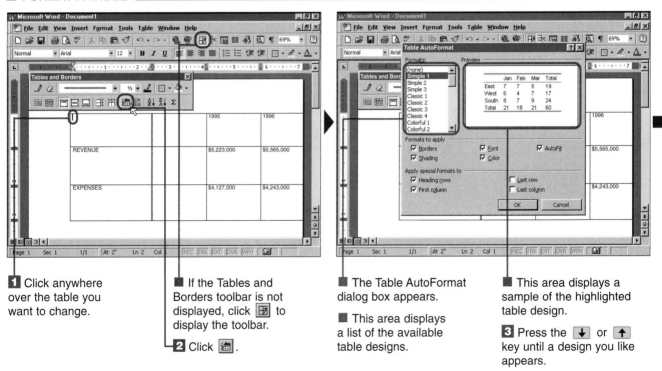

1 Click anywhere over the table you want to change.

■ If the Tables and Borders toolbar is not displayed, click ⊞ to display the toolbar.

2 Click 🖺.

■ The Table AutoFormat dialog box appears.

■ This area displays a list of the available table designs.

■ This area displays a sample of the highlighted table design.

3 Press the ⬇ or ⬆ key until a design you like appears.

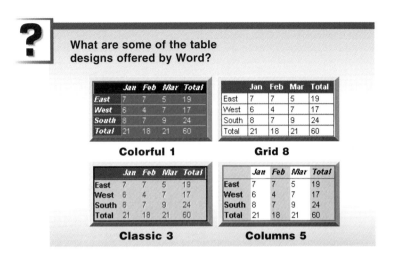

What are some of the table designs offered by Word?

Colorful 1

Grid 8

Classic 3

Columns 5

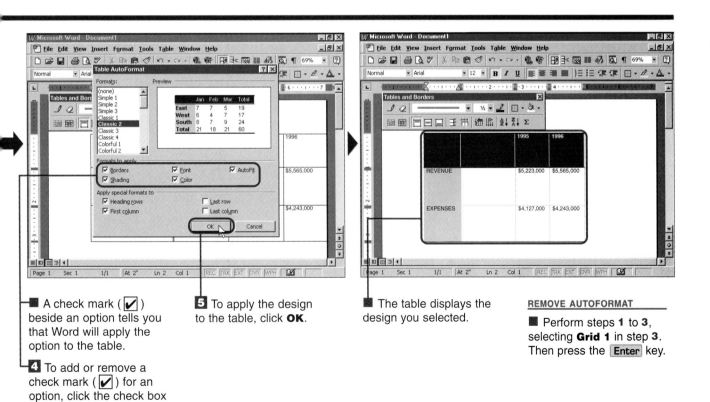

■ A check mark (☑) beside an option tells you that Word will apply the option to the table.

4 To add or remove a check mark (☑) for an option, click the check box beside the option.

5 To apply the design to the table, click **OK**.

■ The table displays the design you selected.

REMOVE AUTOFORMAT

■ Perform steps **1** to **3**, selecting **Grid 1** in step **3**. Then press the **Enter** key.

CHAPTER 13

Work with Graphics

*What can I do to enhance the
appearance of my documents?
Learn how to add colorful graphics
and text effects to your documents.*

ADD A SIMPLE SHAPE

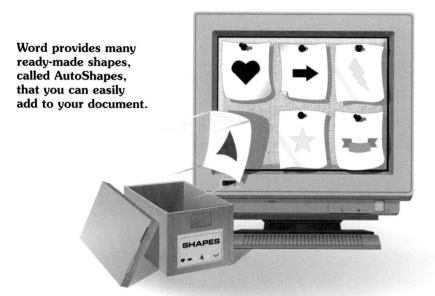

Word provides many ready-made shapes, called AutoShapes, that you can easily add to your document.

Word can only display graphics in the Page Layout and Online Layout views. For information on the four views, refer to page 40.

■ ADD A SIMPLE SHAPE ■

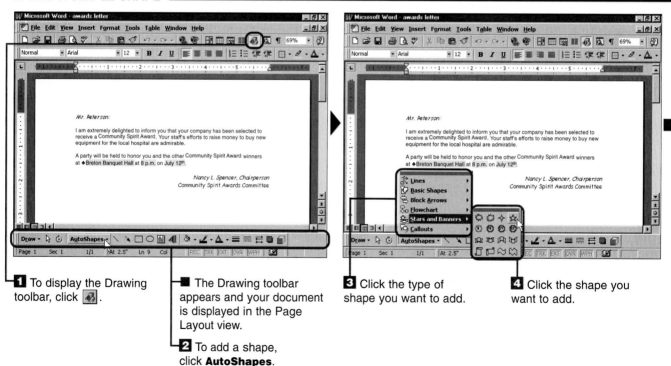

1 To display the Drawing toolbar, click 🔲.

■ The Drawing toolbar appears and your document is displayed in the Page Layout view.

2 To add a shape, click **AutoShapes**.

3 Click the type of shape you want to add.

4 Click the shape you want to add.

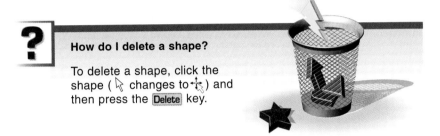

How do I delete a shape?

To delete a shape, click the shape (↖ changes to ✥) and then press the Delete key.

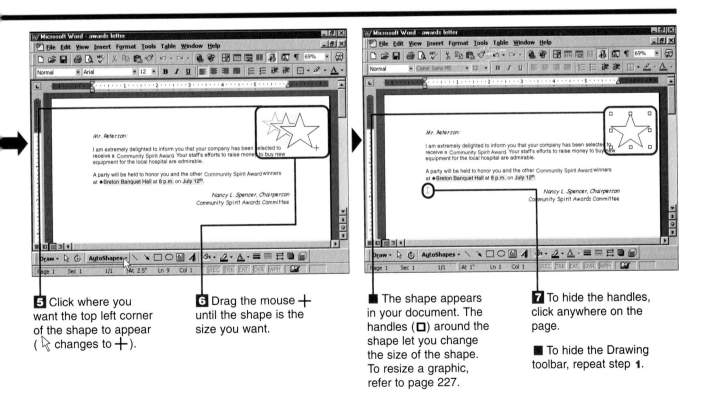

5 Click where you want the top left corner of the shape to appear (↖ changes to +).

6 Drag the mouse + until the shape is the size you want.

■ The shape appears in your document. The handles (□) around the shape let you change the size of the shape. To resize a graphic, refer to page 227.

7 To hide the handles, click anywhere on the page.

■ To hide the Drawing toolbar, repeat step **1**.

ADD CLIP ART OR A PICTURE

You can use professionally designed clip art and pictures that come with Word to enhance your document.

Word can only display graphics in the Page Layout and Online Layout views. For information on the four views, refer to page 40.

■ ADD CLIP ART OR A PICTURE ■

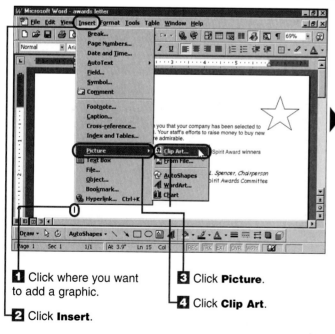

1 Click where you want to add a graphic.

2 Click **Insert**.

3 Click **Picture**.

4 Click **Clip Art**.

■ A dialog box appears if additional graphics are available on the CD-ROM disc identified in this area.

5 To view the additional graphics, insert the CD-ROM disc into your CD-ROM disc drive.

6 Click **OK**.

■ The Microsoft Clip Gallery dialog box appears.

? **What clip art and pictures does Word offer?**

Word offers clip art and pictures of animals, household items, plants, sports and much more.

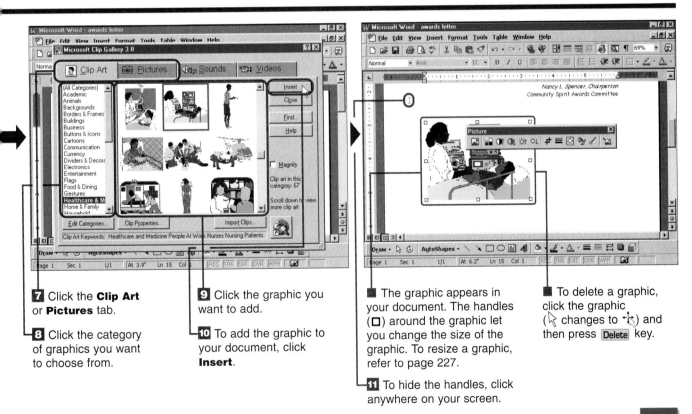

7 Click the **Clip Art** or **Pictures** tab.

8 Click the category of graphics you want to choose from.

9 Click the graphic you want to add.

10 To add the graphic to your document, click **Insert**.

■ The graphic appears in your document. The handles (□) around the graphic let you change the size of the graphic. To resize a graphic, refer to page 227.

11 To hide the handles, click anywhere on your screen.

■ To delete a graphic, click the graphic (⬚ changes to ⬚) and then press Delete key.

ADD A TEXT BOX

You can add a text box to your document. Text boxes allow you to add comments or additional information to a picture or graphic in your document.

Word can only display graphics in the Page Layout and Online Layout views. For information on the four views, refer to page 40.

■ ADD A TEXT BOX

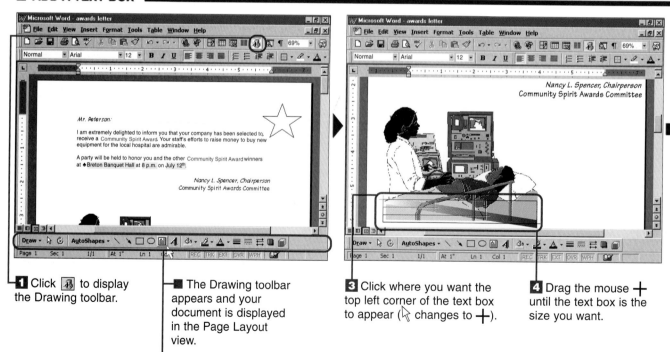

1 Click 🔲 to display the Drawing toolbar.

■ The Drawing toolbar appears and your document is displayed in the Page Layout view.

2 Click 🔲 to add a text box.

3 Click where you want the top left corner of the text box to appear (k changes to ✛).

4 Drag the mouse ✛ until the text box is the size you want.

?

Can I change the appearance of text in a text box?

You can format the text in a text box as you would format any text in your document. You must select the text in the text box before you can change the appearance of the text. To select text, refer to page 12.

■ The text box appears in your document.

5 Type the text you want to appear in the text box.

■ The handles (□) around the text box let you change the size of the text box. To resize a graphic, refer to page 227.

6 To hide the handles, click outside the text box area.

■ To delete a text box, click the text box. Then press the **Delete** key.

ADD A TEXT EFFECT

You can use the
WordArt feature to
add text effects to
your document.

Word can only display
graphics in the Page
Layout and Online
Layout views. For
information on the four
views, refer to page 40.

■ **ADD A TEXT EFFECT**

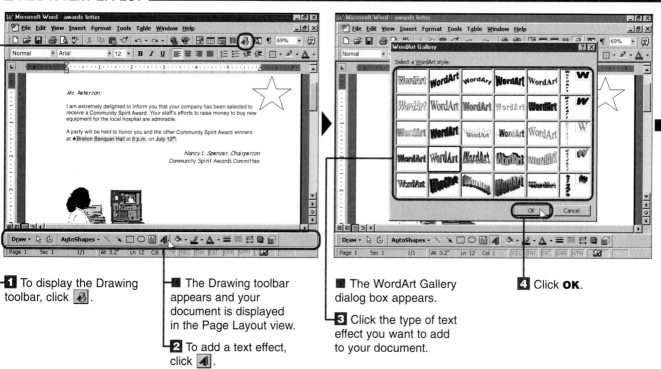

1 To display the Drawing
toolbar, click ✎.

■ The Drawing toolbar
appears and your
document is displayed
in the Page Layout view.

2 To add a text effect,
click ◀.

■ The WordArt Gallery
dialog box appears.

3 Click the type of text
effect you want to add
to your document.

4 Click **OK**.

? How do I delete a text effect?

To delete a text effect, click the text effect (↖ changes to ✥) and then press the Delete key.

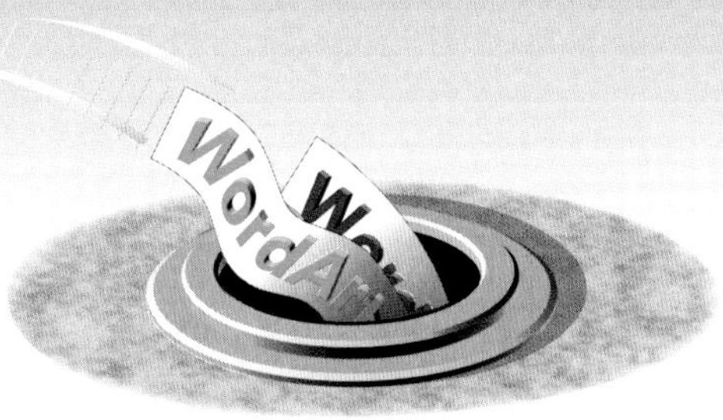

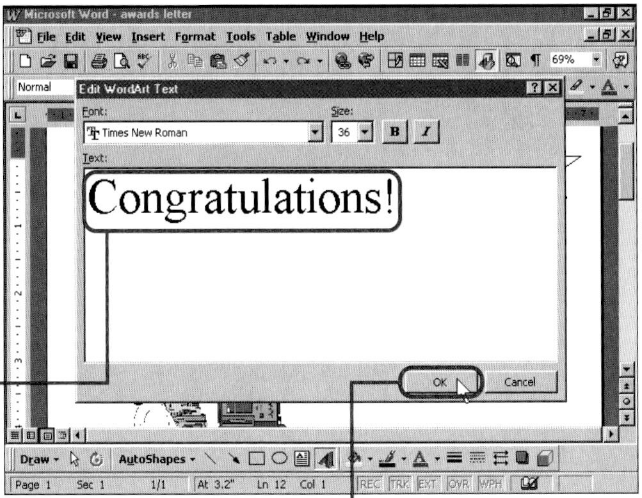

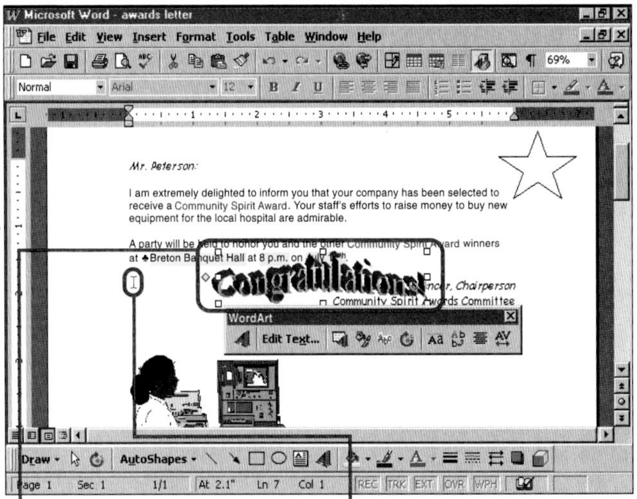

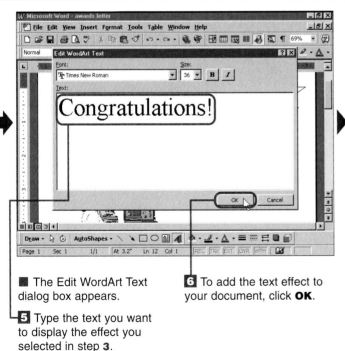

■ The Edit WordArt Text dialog box appears.

5 Type the text you want to display the effect you selected in step **3**.

6 To add the text effect to your document, click **OK**.

■ The text effect appears in your document. The handles (□) around the text effect let you change the size of the text effect. To resize a graphic, refer to page 227.

7 To hide the handles, click outside the text effect area.

■ To hide the Drawing toolbar, repeat step **1**.

MOVE OR RESIZE A GRAPHIC

You can easily change
the location or size of
a graphic in your
document.

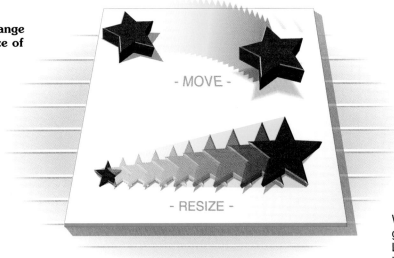

Word can only display
graphics in the Page
Layout and Online
Layout views. For
information on the four
views, refer to page 40.

■ MOVE A GRAPHIC ■

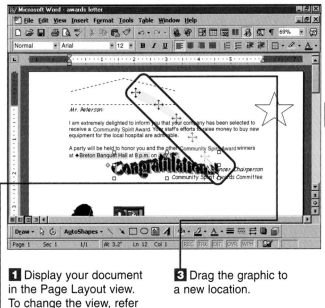

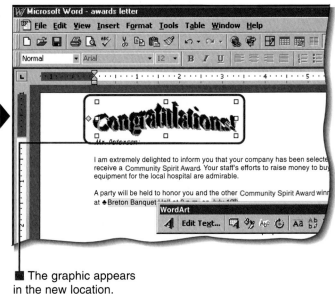

1 Display your document
in the Page Layout view.
To change the view, refer
to page 40.

2 Position the mouse I
over the graphic you want
to move (I changes to ⊹).

3 Drag the graphic to
a new location.

■ The graphic appears
in the new location.

What are the handles (□) that appear around a selected graphic used for?

The handles around a selected graphic let you change the size of the graphic.

▢ Change the height of a graphic.

◼ Change the width of a graphic.

▢ Change the height and width of a graphic at the same time.

■ RESIZE A GRAPHIC ■

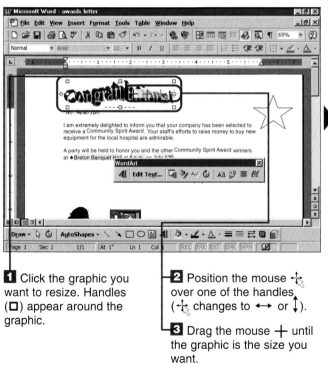

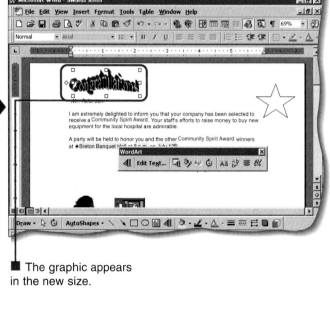

1 Click the graphic you want to resize. Handles (□) appear around the graphic.

2 Position the mouse ⊹ over one of the handles. (⊹ changes to ↔ or ↕).

3 Drag the mouse + until the graphic is the size you want.

◼ The graphic appears in the new size.

CHANGE COLOR OF GRAPHIC

You can easily change the color of a graphic in your document.

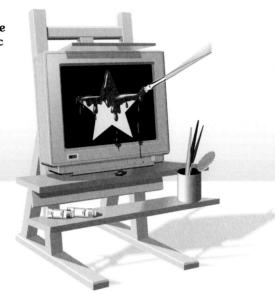

Word can only display graphics in the Page Layout and Online Layout views. For information on the four views, refer to page 40.

■ CHANGE COLOR OF GRAPHIC

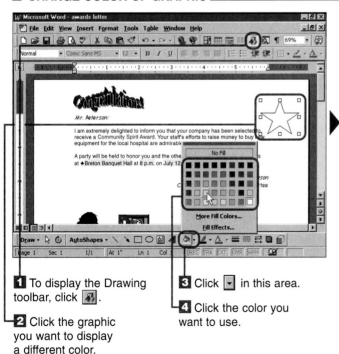

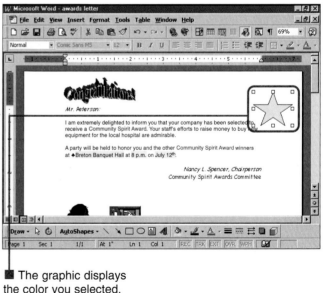

1 To display the Drawing toolbar, click [icon].

2 Click the graphic you want to display a different color.

3 Click [▾] in this area.

4 Click the color you want to use.

■ The graphic displays the color you selected.

MAKE A GRAPHIC 3-D

You can make a graphic appear three dimensional.

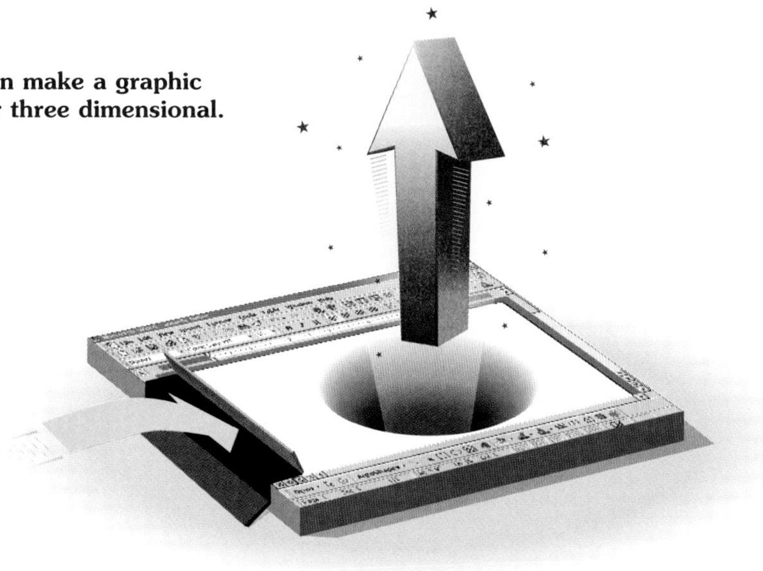

Word can only display graphics in the Page Layout and Online Layout views. For information on the four views, refer to page 40.

MAKE A GRAPHIC 3-D

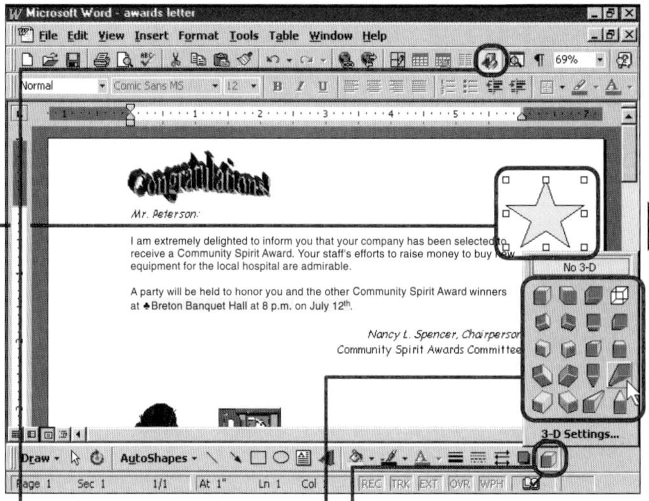

1 To display the Drawing toolbar, click .

2 Click the graphic you want to appear in 3-D.

3 Click .

4 Click the 3-D effect you want to use.

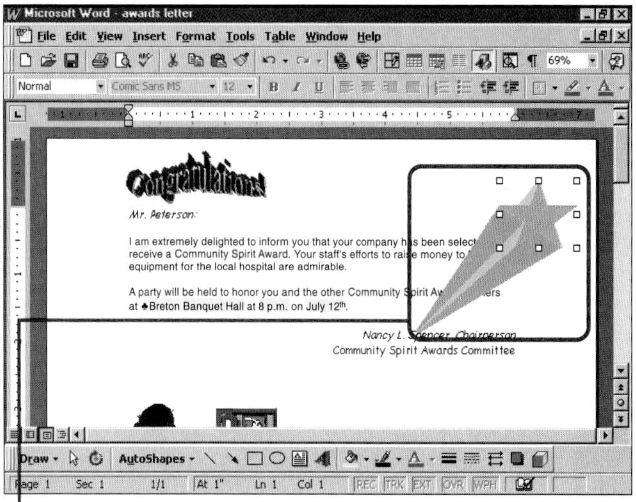

■ The graphic appears in 3-D.

WRAP TEXT AROUND A GRAPHIC

You can easily wrap text
around a graphic in your
document.

Word can only display
graphics in the Page Layout
and Online Layout views.
For information on the four
views, refer to page 40.

■ WRAP TEXT AROUND A GRAPHIC ■

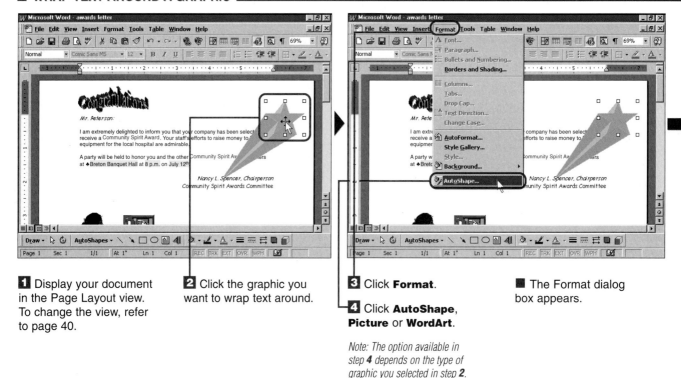

1 Display your document
in the Page Layout view.
To change the view, refer
to page 40.

2 Click the graphic you
want to wrap text around.

3 Click **Format**.

4 Click **AutoShape**,
Picture or **WordArt**.

*Note: The option available in
step **4** depends on the type of
graphic you selected in step **2**.*

■ The Format dialog
box appears.

How can I wrap text around a graphic?

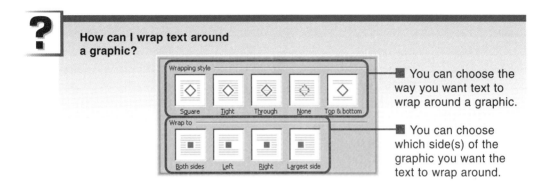

■ You can choose the way you want text to wrap around a graphic.

■ You can choose which side(s) of the graphic you want the text to wrap around.

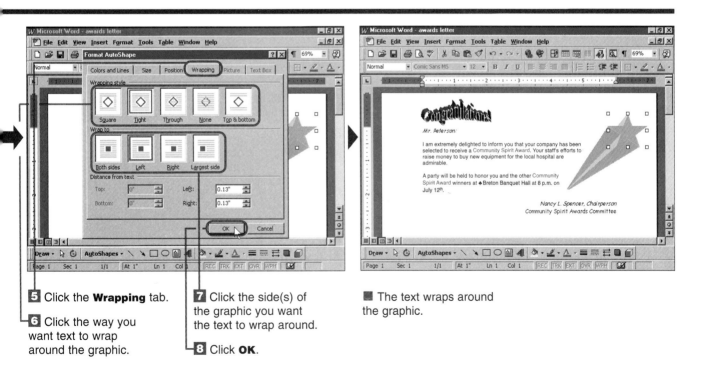

5 Click the **Wrapping** tab.

6 Click the way you want text to wrap around the graphic.

7 Click the side(s) of the graphic you want the text to wrap around.

8 Click **OK**.

■ The text wraps around the graphic.

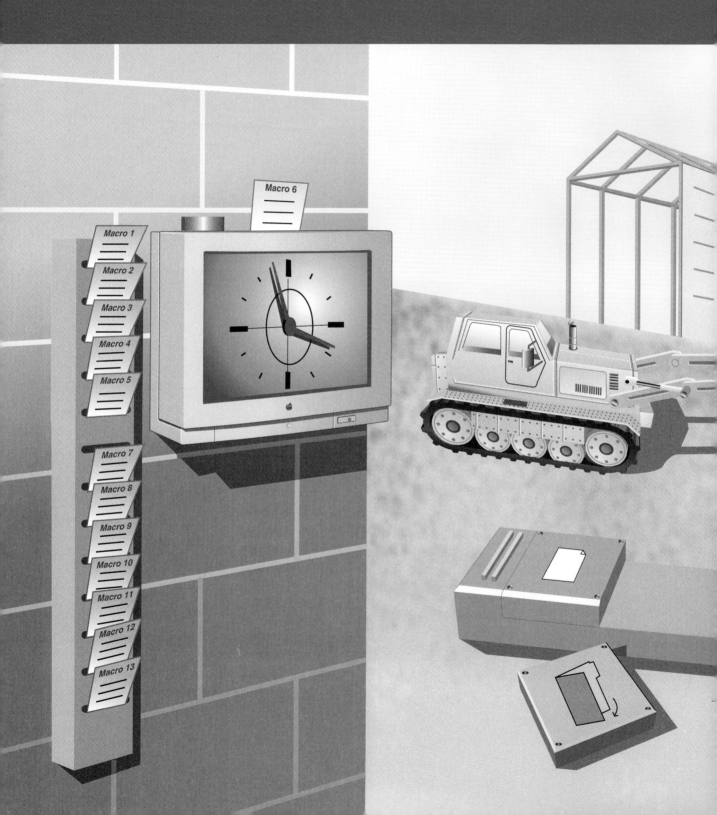

Time-saving Features

Would you like to spend less time creating your documents? In this chapter you will learn how to work with some of the time-saving tools Word provides such as macros, templates and wizards.

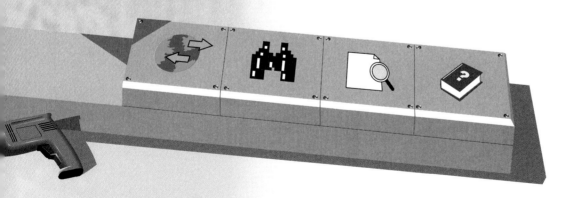

USING TEMPLATES AND WIZARDS

You can use templates and wizards to save time when creating many common types of documents.

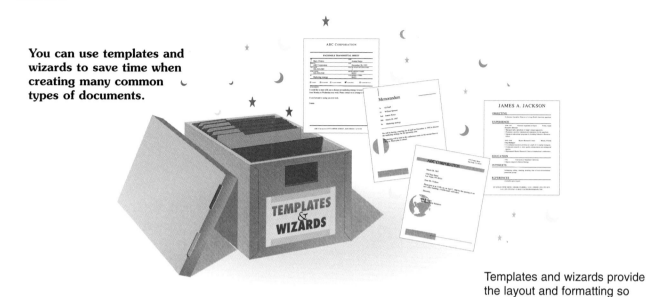

Templates and wizards provide the layout and formatting so you can concentrate on the content of your document.

■ USING TEMPLATES AND WIZARDS

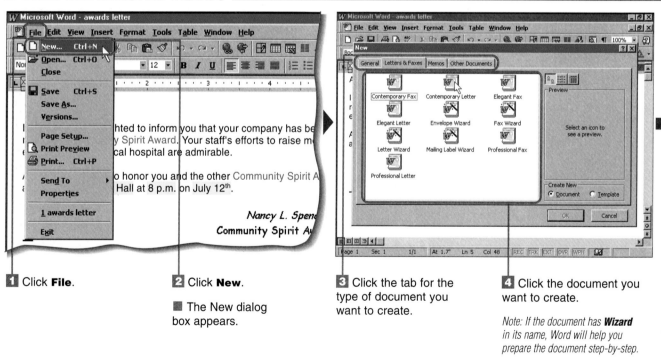

1 Click **File**.

2 Click **New**.

■ The New dialog box appears.

3 Click the tab for the type of document you want to create.

4 Click the document you want to create.

Note: If the document has **Wizard** in its name, Word will help you prepare the document step-by-step.

? What is the difference between a template and a wizard?

Template

When you select a template, a document immediately appears with areas for you to fill in your personalized information.

Wizard

When you select a wizard, you will be asked a series of questions. The wizard uses your answers to help complete the document.

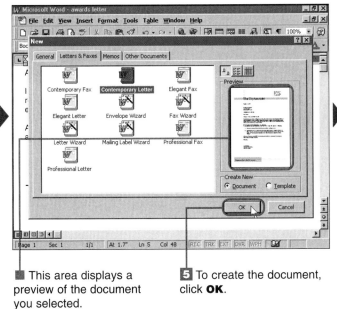

■ This area displays a preview of the document you selected.

5 To create the document, click **OK**.

■ The document appears on your screen.

Note: If you selected a wizard in step 4, Word will ask you a series of questions before creating the document.

6 Type information where required to complete the document.

CREATE A TEMPLATE

You can create a template from any document. Using a template you have created helps you quickly create other documents that use the same formatting, page settings and even text.

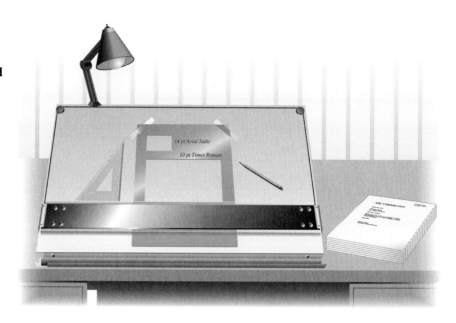

■ **CREATE A TEMPLATE** ■

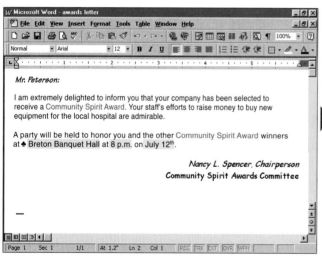

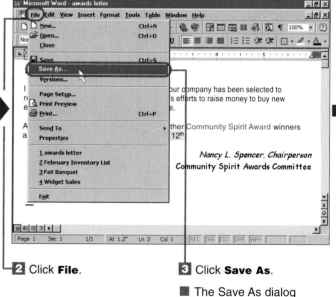

1 Open the document you want to use as the basis for the template. To open a document, refer to page 30.

2 Click **File**.

3 Click **Save As**.

■ The Save As dialog box appears.

How do I use a template I created?

When you store your template in the Templates folder, the template will appear on the General tab in the New dialog box. For more information on using templates, refer to page 234.

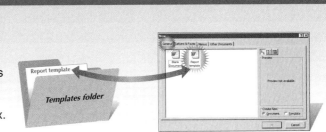

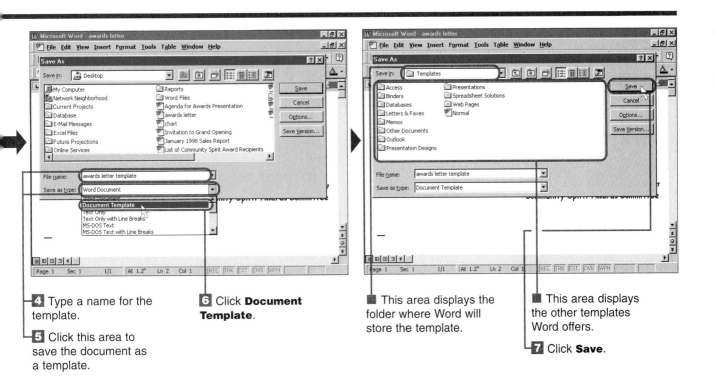

4 Type a name for the template.

5 Click this area to save the document as a template.

6 Click **Document Template**.

■ This area displays the folder where Word will store the template.

■ This area displays the other templates Word offers.

7 Click **Save**.

RECORD A MACRO

A macro saves you time
by combining a series of
commands into a single
command.

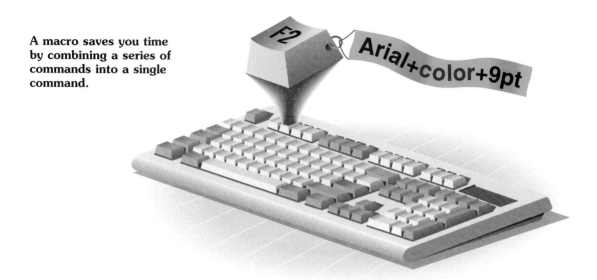

■ RECORD A MACRO ■

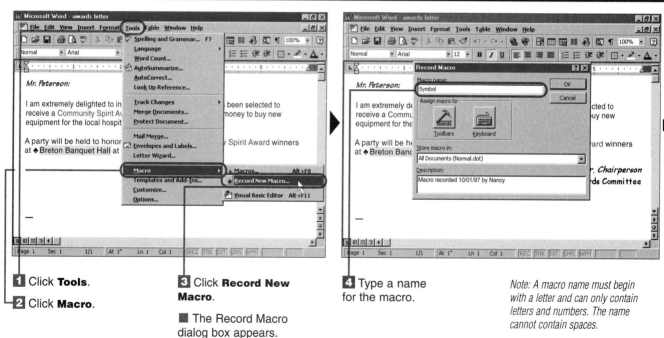

1 Click **Tools**.

2 Click **Macro**.

3 Click **Record New Macro**.

■ The Record Macro dialog box appears.

4 Type a name for the macro.

Note: A macro name must begin with a letter and can only contain letters and numbers. The name cannot contain spaces.

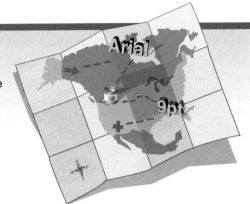

Should I practice before I record a macro?

You should plan and practice all the actions you want the macro to perform before you record the macro. Word will record any mistakes or corrections you make when recording.

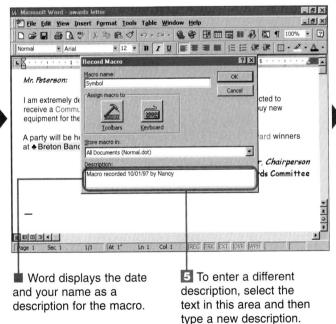

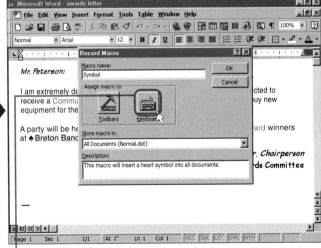

■ Word displays the date and your name as a description for the macro.

5 To enter a different description, select the text in this area and then type a new description.

6 Click **Keyboard** to assign a keyboard shortcut to the macro.

■ The Customize Keyboard dialog box appears.

CONTINUED

RECORD A MACRO

Macros are ideal for tasks you perform over and over.

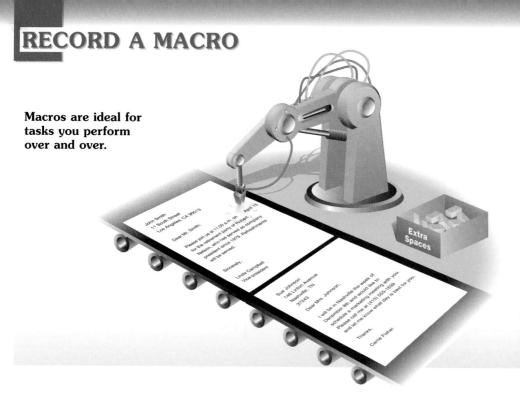

For example, you can create a macro that will remove extra spaces from your documents.

RECORD A MACRO (CONTINUED)

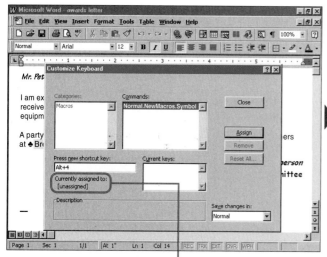

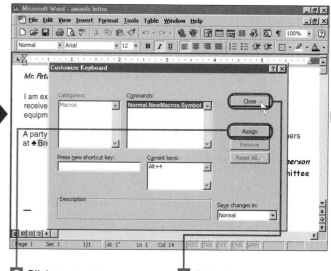

7 To specify the keyboard shortcut you want to use, press and hold down the **Alt** key as you press a letter or number key. Then release the **Alt** key.

■ This area displays the word **[unassigned]**.

*Note: If the word **[unassigned]** is not displayed, the keyboard shortcut is already assigned. Press the **◆Backspace** key to delete the shortcut and then repeat step 7, using a different letter or number.*

8 Click **Assign** to assign the keyboard shortcut to the macro.

9 Click **Close**.

Why would I use a macro?

Macros can help speed up many repetitive tasks, such as editing and formatting text. Macros are also useful for quickly inserting specific text or special characters into your documents.

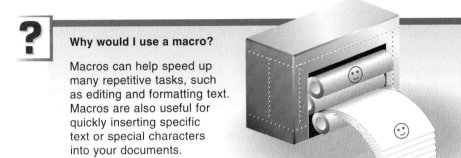

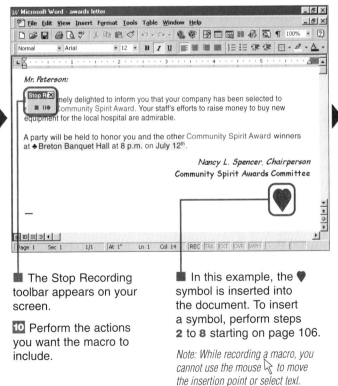

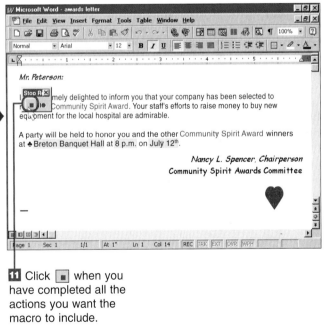

■ The Stop Recording toolbar appears on your screen.

🔟 Perform the actions you want the macro to include.

■ In this example, the ♥ symbol is inserted into the document. To insert a symbol, perform steps 2 to 8 starting on page 106.

Note: While recording a macro, you cannot use the mouse ⬚ to move the insertion point or select text.

11 Click ■ when you have completed all the actions you want the macro to include.

RUN A MACRO

When you run a macro,
Word automatically
performs the series
of commands you
recorded.

■ RUN A MACRO

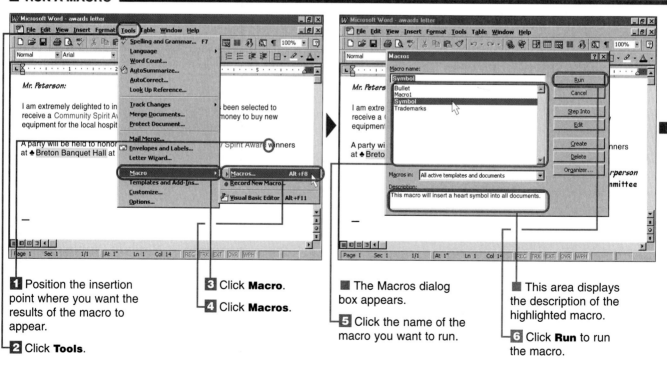

1 Position the insertion
point where you want the
results of the macro to
appear.

2 Click **Tools**.

3 Click **Macro**.

4 Click **Macros**.

■ The Macros dialog
box appears.

5 Click the name of the
macro you want to run.

■ This area displays
the description of the
highlighted macro.

6 Click **Run** to run
the macro.

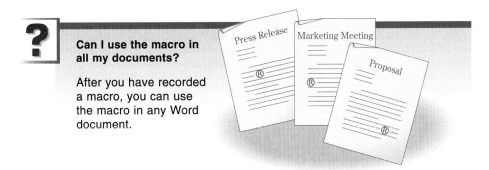

Can I use the macro in all my documents?

After you have recorded a macro, you can use the macro in any Word document.

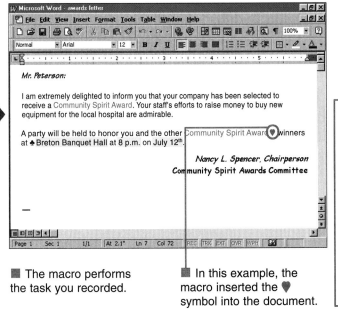

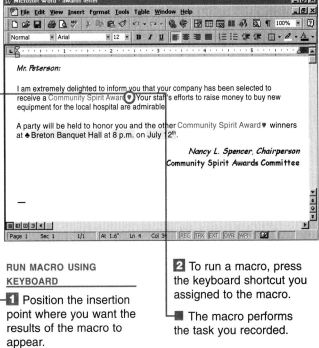

■ The macro performs the task you recorded.

■ In this example, the macro inserted the ♥ symbol into the document.

RUN MACRO USING KEYBOARD

■1 Position the insertion point where you want the results of the macro to appear.

■2 To run a macro, press the keyboard shortcut you assigned to the macro.

■ The macro performs the task you recorded.

CUSTOMIZE THE TOOLBARS

You can customize the toolbars to help you work more efficiently. You can remove buttons you no longer use and change the order of buttons on any toolbar.

■ REMOVE A BUTTON ■

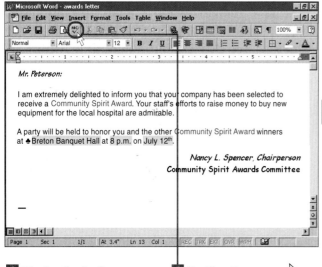

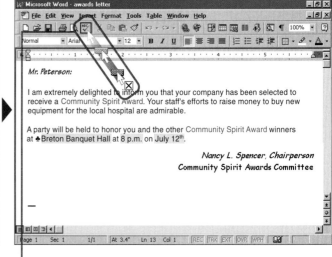

1 Display the toolbar you want to customize. To display a toolbar, refer to page 44.

2 Position the mouse over the button you want to remove.

3 Press and hold down the `Alt` key.

4 Still holding down the `Alt` key, drag the button downward off the toolbar. Then release the `Alt` key and the mouse button.

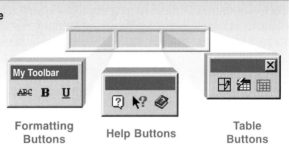

Why should I reorganize the buttons on a toolbar?

You should reorganize the buttons on a toolbar to group buttons for related tasks together. This may make it easier to find the tools you need.

Formatting Buttons

Help Buttons

Table Buttons

■ MOVE A BUTTON

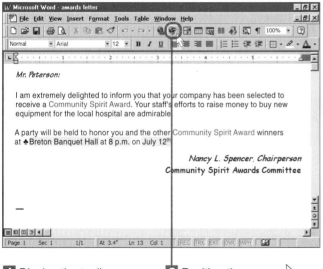

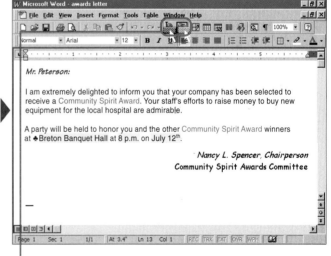

1 Display the toolbar you want to customize. To display a toolbar, refer to page 44.

2 Position the mouse over the button you want to move.

3 Press and hold down the Alt key.

4 Still holding down the Alt key, drag the button to the new location. A line indicates where the button will appear. Release the Alt key and the mouse button.

CONTINUED

CUSTOMIZE THE TOOLBARS

You can add buttons to a toolbar to provide quick access to the commands you use most often.

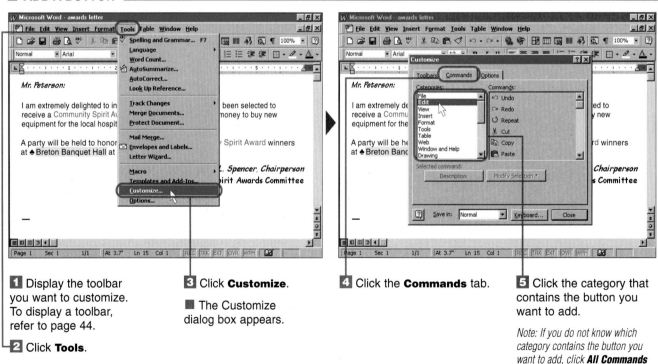

ADD A BUTTON

1 Display the toolbar you want to customize. To display a toolbar, refer to page 44.

2 Click **Tools**.

3 Click **Customize**.

■ The Customize dialog box appears.

4 Click the **Commands** tab.

5 Click the category that contains the button you want to add.

*Note: If you do not know which category contains the button you want to add, click **All Commands** to display all the buttons.*

What types of buttons can I add to a toolbar?

Word offers hundreds of buttons from several different categories. Each category provides tools to help you perform a specific type of task.

For example, the Format category offers many tools that you can use to format text and paragraphs in your documents, such as line spacing, font options and underline styles.

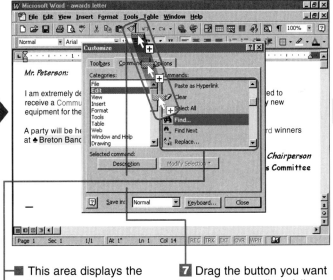

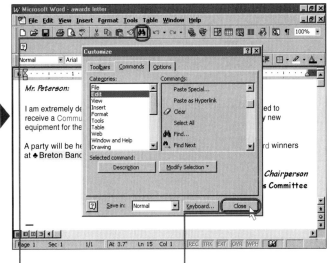

■ This area displays the buttons in the category you selected.

6 Position the mouse over the button you want to add.

7 Drag the button you want to add to the toolbar. A line indicates where the button will appear.

■ The button appears on the toolbar.

8 Click **Close** when you finish adding buttons to the toolbar.

CONTINUED

CUSTOMIZE THE TOOLBARS

You can change the image that
appears on a toolbar button.
Changing the image can help
draw attention to an
important button
on a toolbar.

Word offers several
interesting and fun images
that you can use.

CUSTOMIZE A BUTTON

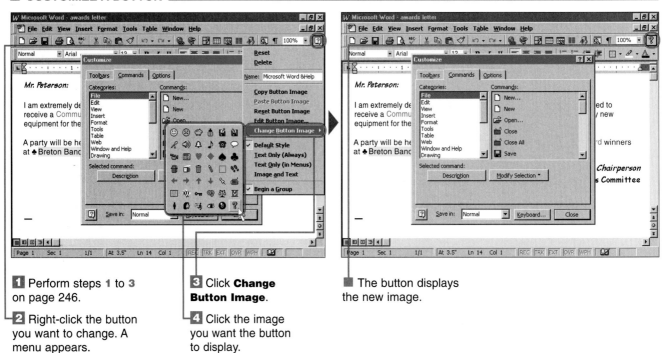

1 Perform steps 1 to 3
on page 246.

2 Right-click the button
you want to change. A
menu appears.

3 Click **Change
Button Image**.

4 Click the image
you want the button
to display.

■ The button displays
the new image.

You can instantly reverse
all the changes you
made to a toolbar
and return the
toolbar to its
original settings.

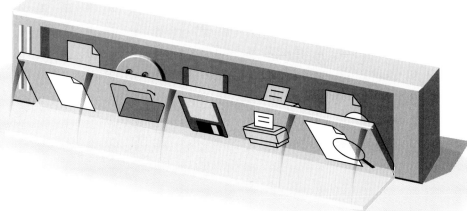

RESET A TOOLBAR

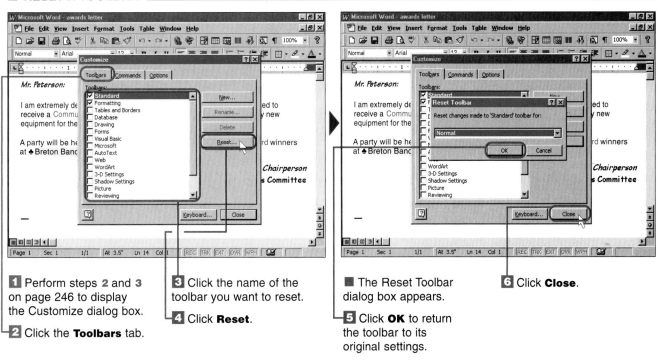

1 Perform steps **2** and **3**
on page 246 to display
the Customize dialog box.

2 Click the **Toolbars** tab.

3 Click the name of the
toolbar you want to reset.

4 Click **Reset**.

■ The Reset Toolbar
dialog box appears.

5 Click **OK** to return
the toolbar to its
original settings.

6 Click **Close**.

CREATE A NEW TOOLBAR

You can create a new toolbar containing the buttons and commands you use most often.

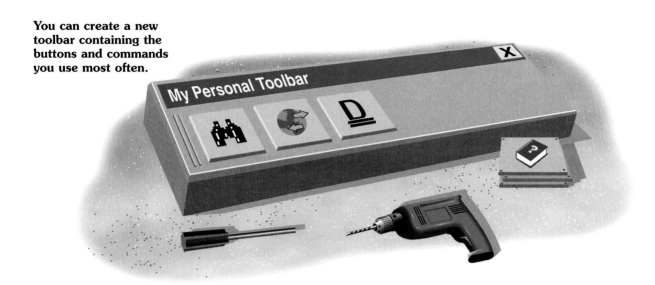

■ CREATE A NEW TOOLBAR

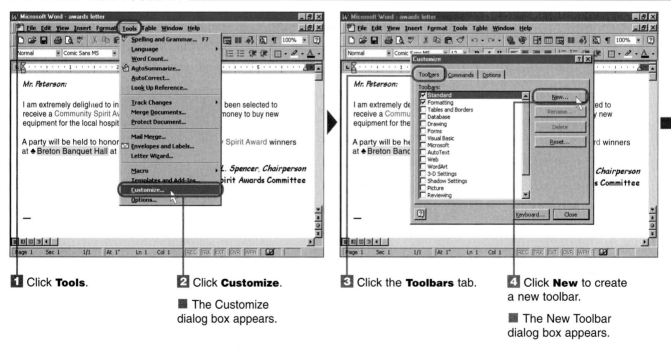

1 Click **Tools**.

2 Click **Customize**.

■ The Customize dialog box appears.

3 Click the **Toolbars** tab.

4 Click **New** to create a new toolbar.

■ The New Toolbar dialog box appears.

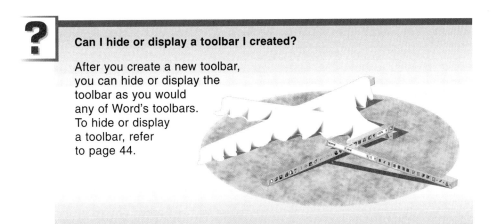

? **Can I hide or display a toolbar I created?**

After you create a new toolbar, you can hide or display the toolbar as you would any of Word's toolbars. To hide or display a toolbar, refer to page 44.

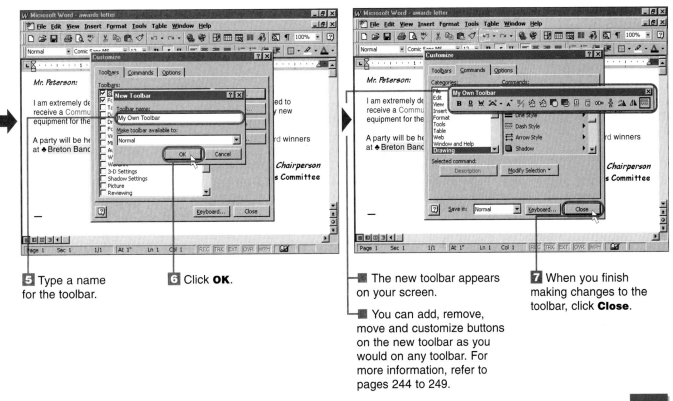

5 Type a name for the toolbar.

6 Click **OK**.

■ The new toolbar appears on your screen.

■ You can add, remove, move and customize buttons on the new toolbar as you would on any toolbar. For more information, refer to pages 244 to 249.

7 When you finish making changes to the toolbar, click **Close**.

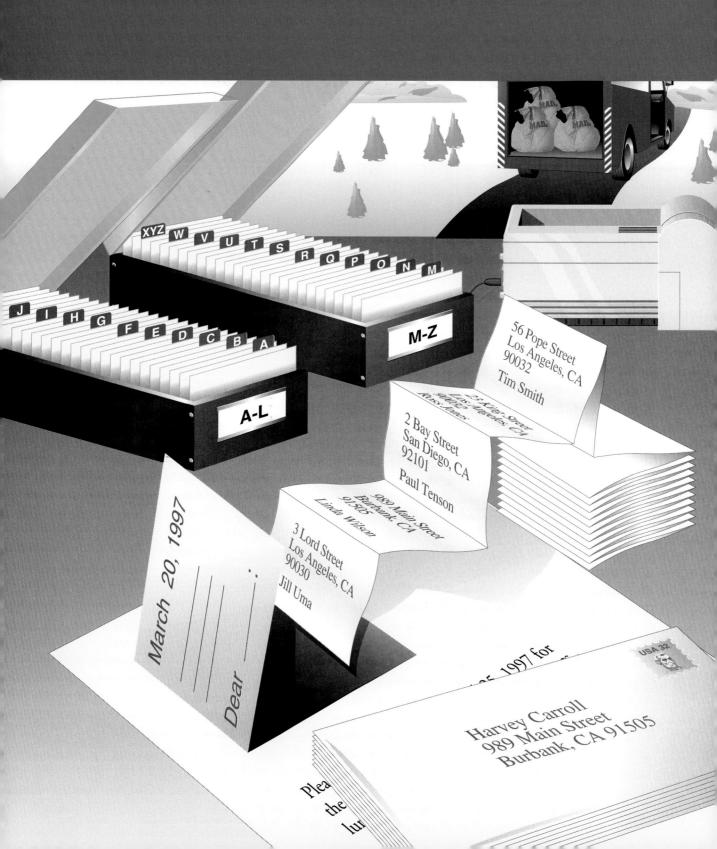

CHAPTER 15

Mail Merge

Is there an efficient way to create personalized letters and labels for my customers? Word offers a Mail Merge feature to help you complete these tasks quickly and easily.

INTRODUCTION TO MAIL MERGE

You can use the
Mail Merge feature
to quickly produce
a personalized letter
for each customer
on a mailing list.

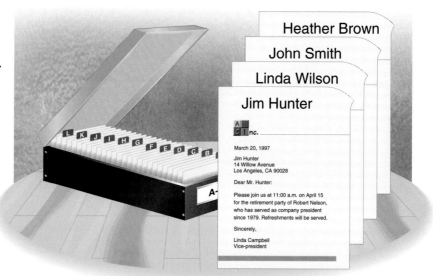

Create a Main Document

A main document is a letter you
want to send to each customer
on your mailing list.

Create a Data Source

A data source contains the information that
changes in each letter, such as the name
and address of each customer. You only
need to create a data source once. After
you create a data source, you can use
the data source for every mailing.

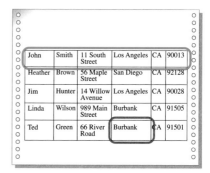

All the information for
one customer is called
a **record**.

Each piece of information
about the customer is called
a **field**.

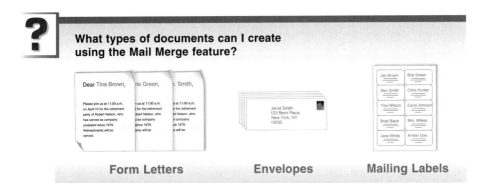

? What types of documents can I create using the Mail Merge feature?

Form Letters   **Envelopes**   **Mailing Labels**

STEP THREE

Complete the Main Document

You must insert special instructions into the main document. These instructions tell Word where to place the personalized information from the data source.

{{FirstName}} {{LastName}}
{{Address1}}
{{City}}, {{State}} {{PostalCode}}

{{Greeting}}

STEP FOUR

Merge the Main Document and Data Source

You combine, or merge, the main document and the data source to create a personalized letter for each customer on your mailing list.

Word replaces the special instructions in the main document with the personalized information from the data source.

CREATE A MAIN DOCUMENT

The main document contains the text that remains the same in each letter.

A main document can be a new document or a document you previously created.

■ **CREATE A MAIN DOCUMENT** ═══════════════════════════

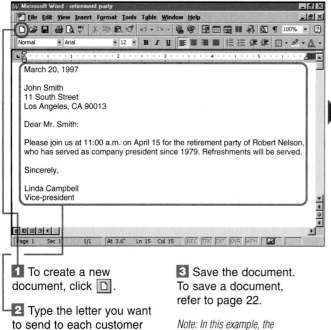

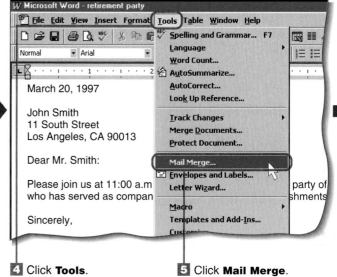

1 To create a new document, click 🗋.

2 Type the letter you want to send to each customer on your mailing list. Include the personalized information for one customer.

3 Save the document. To save a document, refer to page 22.

Note: In this example, the document was named **retirement party**.

4 Click **Tools**.

5 Click **Mail Merge**.

When should I check my main document for errors?

Make sure you carefully review the text in your main document right after you type the document. Check for spelling and grammar errors and review the layout and formatting of the document. Remember that the document will be read by every person on your mailing list.

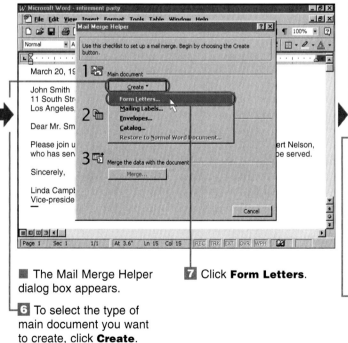

■ The Mail Merge Helper dialog box appears.

6 To select the type of main document you want to create, click **Create**.

7 Click **Form Letters**.

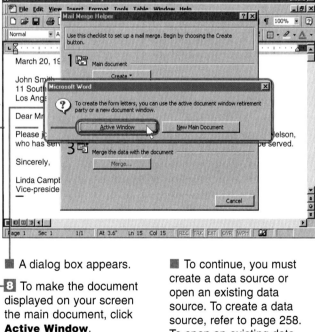

■ A dialog box appears.

8 To make the document displayed on your screen the main document, click **Active Window**.

■ To continue, you must create a data source or open an existing data source. To create a data source, refer to page 258. To open an existing data source, refer to page 264.

CREATE A DATA SOURCE

The data source contains the information that changes in each letter, such as the name and address of each customer.

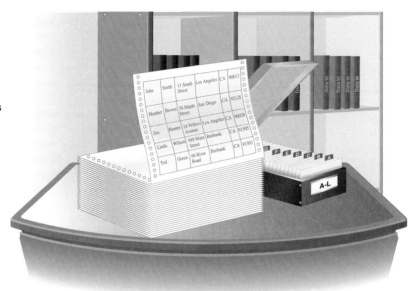

You only need to create a data source once. To use an existing data source, refer to page 264.

■ CREATE A DATA SOURCE

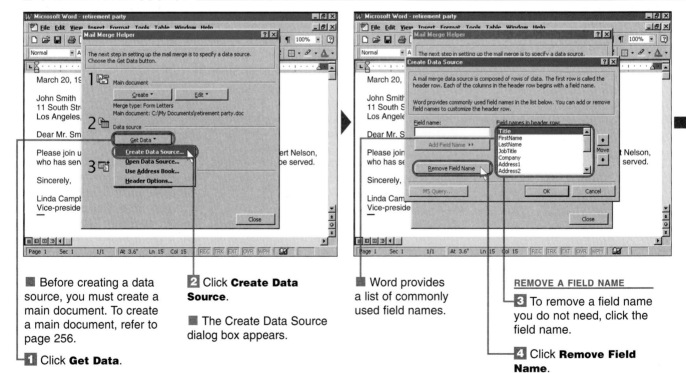

■ Before creating a data source, you must create a main document. To create a main document, refer to page 256.

1 Click **Get Data**.

2 Click **Create Data Source**.

■ The Create Data Source dialog box appears.

■ Word provides a list of commonly used field names.

REMOVE A FIELD NAME

3 To remove a field name you do not need, click the field name.

4 Click **Remove Field Name**.

?

What is a field name?

A field name is a name given to a category of information, such as **LastName** or **City**.

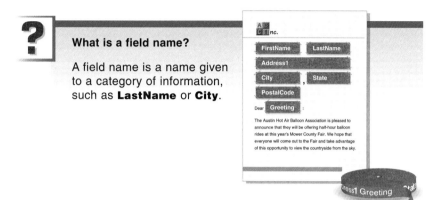

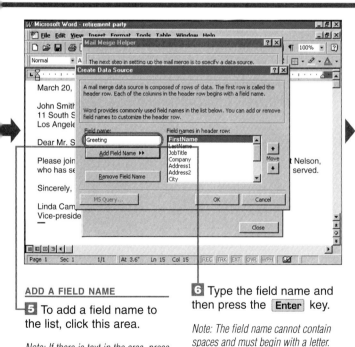

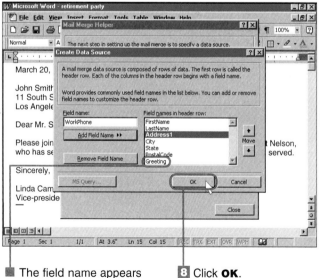

ADD A FIELD NAME

5 To add a field name to the list, click this area.

Note: If there is text in the area, press the **Delete** *or* **+Backspace** *key until you have removed all the text.*

6 Type the field name and then press the **Enter** key.

Note: The field name cannot contain spaces and must begin with a letter.

■ The field name appears in the list.

7 Remove and add field names until the list displays the field names you need.

8 Click **OK**.

CONTINUED

CREATE A DATA SOURCE

After you save the data
source, you can enter
the information for
each customer.

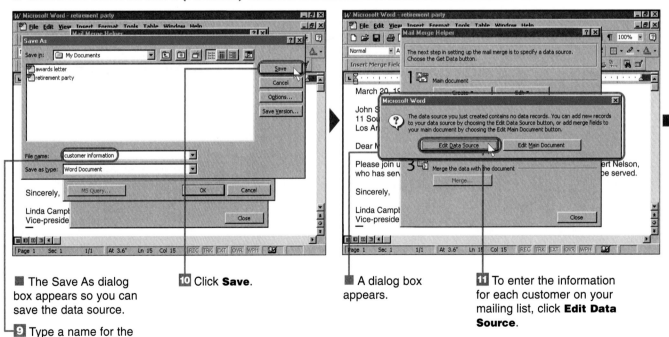

■ The Save As dialog
box appears so you can
save the data source.

9 Type a name for the
data source.

10 Click **Save**.

■ A dialog box
appears.

11 To enter the information
for each customer on your
mailing list, click **Edit Data
Source**.

?

How can I browse through the customer information I have entered?

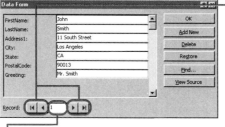

1 To browse through the customers, click one of the following options:

⏮ Display the first customer.

◀ Display the previous customer.

▶ Display the next customer.

⏭ Display the last customer.

■ This area displays the number of the customer that is currently displayed.

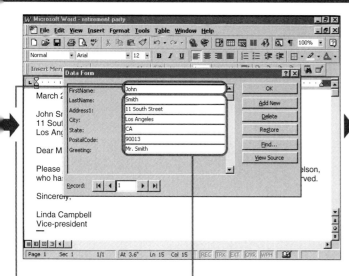

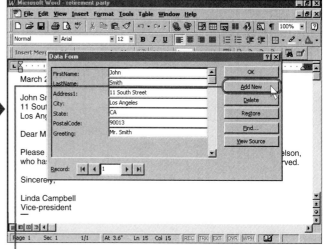

■ The Data Form dialog box appears, displaying areas where you can enter the information for one customer.

12 Type the information that corresponds to the first area. To move to the next area, press the **Tab** key.

13 Repeat step **12** until you finish typing all the information for the customer.

14 To enter the information for the next customer, click **Add New**.

15 Repeat steps **12** to **14** for each customer on your mailing list.

CONTINUED

CREATE A DATA SOURCE

You can have Word display
a table containing all the
customer information
you have entered.

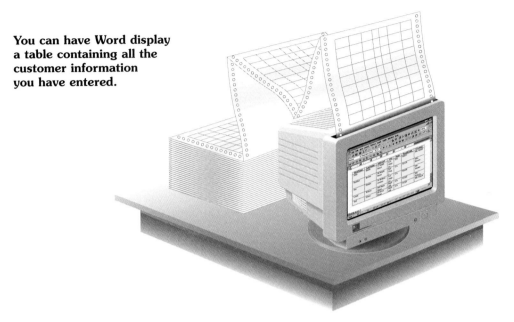

■ CREATE A DATA SOURCE (CONTINUED)

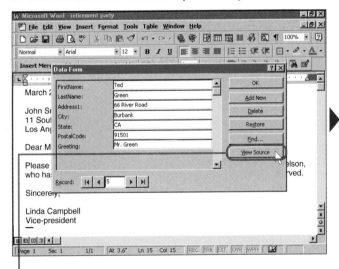

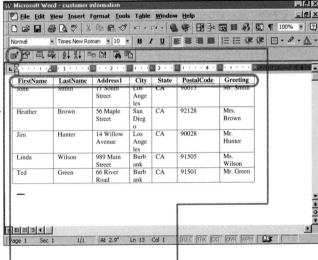

■16 When you have entered
the information for all your
customers, click **View
Source**.

■ The information
you entered appears
in a table.

■ The first row in the table
contains the field names.
Each of the following rows
contains the information for
one customer.

*Note: Text that does not fit on one
line in the table will appear on one
line when you print the letters.*

■ If you want to add
or change customer
information, click 🖳
to display the Data
Form dialog box.

Can I use the data source with other letters?

Once you create a data source, you can use the data source for any future mailings.

Before using a data source with a new letter, you may want to update your customer information. You can open, edit and save a data source as you would any document.

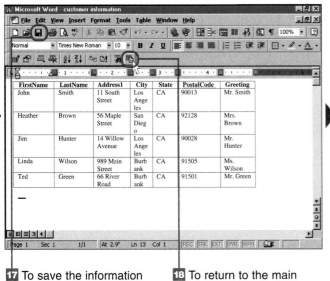

17 To save the information you entered, click 🖫.

18 To return to the main document, click 🖳.

■ The main document appears on your screen.

■ To continue, you must complete the main document. To complete the main document, refer to page 266.

OPEN AN EXISTING DATA SOURCE

You can use a data
source you previously
created for all of your
mailings.

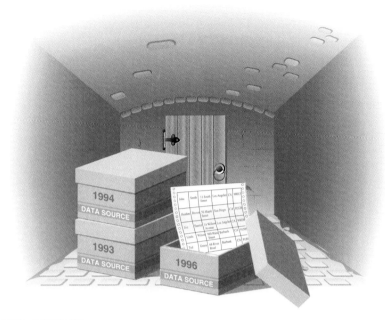

OPEN AN EXISTING DATA SOURCE

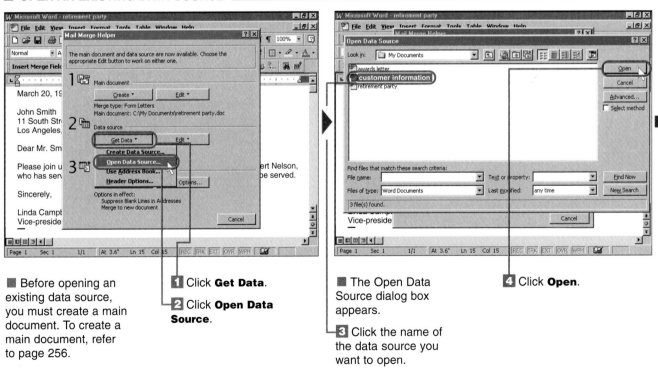

■ Before opening an
existing data source,
you must create a main
document. To create a
main document, refer
to page 256.

1 Click **Get Data**.

2 Click **Open Data Source**.

■ The Open Data
Source dialog box
appears.

3 Click the name of
the data source you
want to open.

4 Click **Open**.

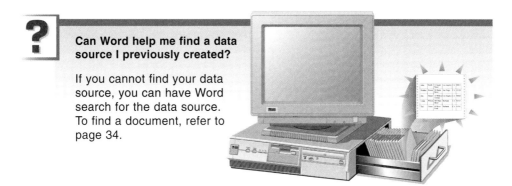

Can Word help me find a data source I previously created?

If you cannot find your data source, you can have Word search for the data source. To find a document, refer to page 34.

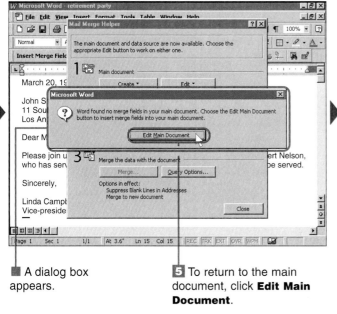

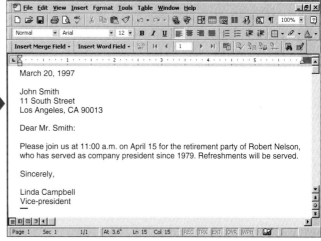

■ A dialog box appears.

5 To return to the main document, click **Edit Main Document**.

■ The main document appears on your screen.

■ To continue, you must complete the main document. To complete the main document, refer to page 266.

COMPLETE THE MAIN DOCUMENT

You must insert special
instructions to complete
the main document.
These instructions tell
Word where to place the
personalized information
that changes for each
customer.

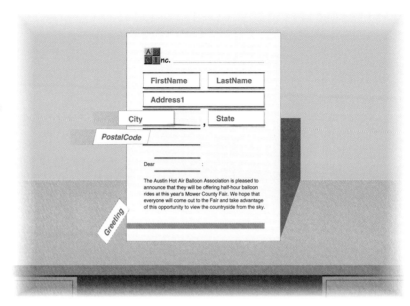

■ COMPLETE THE MAIN DOCUMENT ■

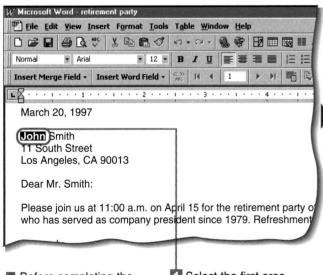

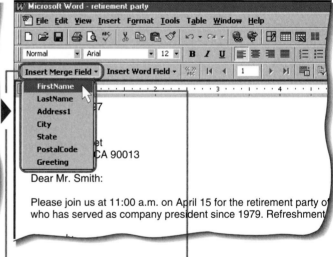

■ Before completing the
main document, you must
create a main document.
To create a main document,
refer to page 256.

1 Select the first area
of text that you want to
change in each letter.
Do not select any spaces
before or after the text.
To select text, refer to
page 12.

2 To display a list of field
names, click **Insert Merge
Field**.

*Note: The field names that appear
depend on the field names you
specified when you created the
data source.*

3 Click the field name
that corresponds to the
text you selected in
step **1**.

After I complete the main document, can I see an example of how my letters will look?

You can temporarily replace the field names in the main document with the information for one customer.

1 Click ⟪⟫.

▓ To view the field names again, repeat step **1**.

▓ The field name replaces the text you selected.

4 Repeat steps **1** to **3** for all the text you want to change in each letter.

5 To save the document, click 🔲.

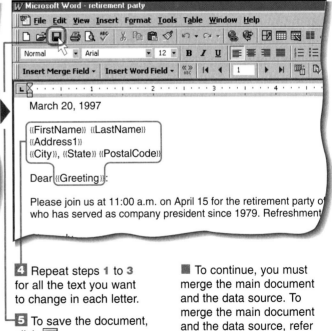

▓ To continue, you must merge the main document and the data source. To merge the main document and the data source, refer to page 268.

MERGE THE MAIN DOCUMENT AND DATA SOURCE

You can combine the main document and the data source to create a personalized letter for each customer on your mailing list.

MERGE THE MAIN DOCUMENT AND DATA SOURCE

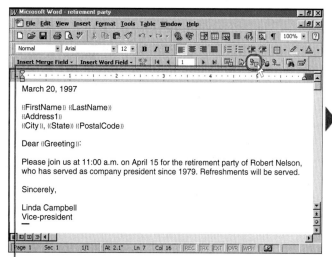

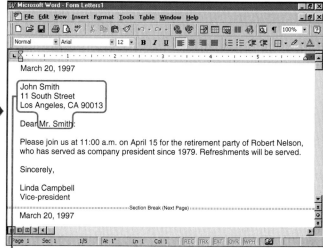

1 To merge the main document and the data source, click ▣.

■ Word replaces the field names in the main document with the corresponding information from the data source. This creates a personalized letter for each customer.

Note: You can edit the letters as you would edit any document. You may wish to add personalized comments to some letters.

Should I save the merged document?

To conserve hard drive space, do not save the merged document. You can easily recreate the merged document at any time by opening the main document and then performing step 1 on page 268.

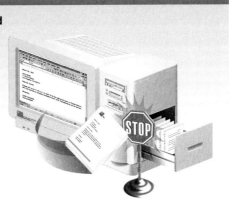

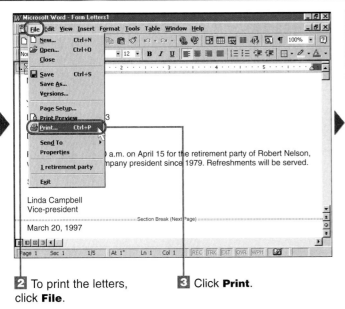

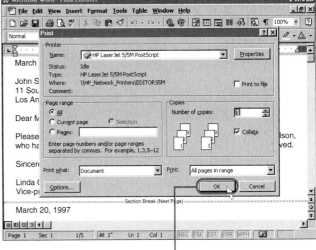

2 To print the letters, click **File**.

3 Click **Print**.

■ The Print dialog box appears.

4 Click **OK**.

USING MAIL MERGE TO PRINT LABELS

You can use the Mail Merge feature to print a mailing label for every customer on your mailing list.

■ USING MAIL MERGE TO PRINT LABELS ■

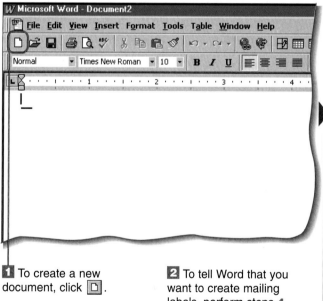

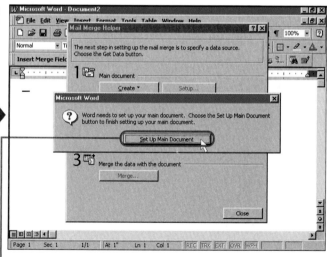

1 To create a new document, click ☐.

2 To tell Word that you want to create mailing labels, perform steps **4** to **8** starting on page 256, selecting **Mailing Labels** in step **7**.

3 To open an existing data source, perform steps **1** to **4** on page 264.

4 To set up the labels, click **Set Up Main Document**.

■ The Label Options dialog box appears.

How can I tell which label product I am using?

You can check your label packaging to determine which label product to select in step **6** below.

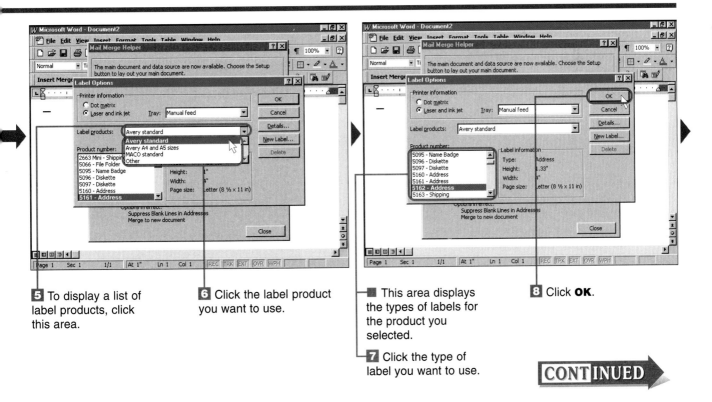

5 To display a list of label products, click this area.

6 Click the label product you want to use.

■ This area displays the types of labels for the product you selected.

7 Click the type of label you want to use.

8 Click **OK**.

CONTINUED

USING MAIL MERGE TO PRINT LABELS

You must insert special instructions to tell Word where to place the personalized information that will change in each label.

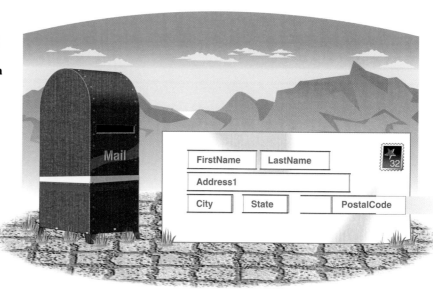

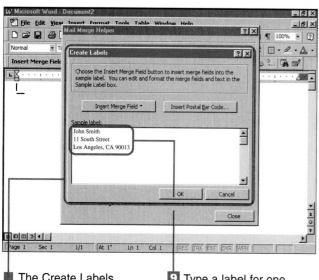

■ The Create Labels dialog box appears.

9 Type a label for one of the customers on your mailing list.

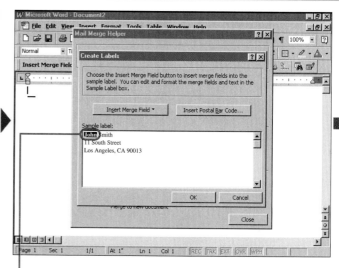

10 Select the first area of text that you want to change in each label. Do not select any spaces before or after the text. To select text, refer to page 12.

?

How can I use the labels that I print using the Mail Merge feature?

You can use the labels for items such as envelopes, packages, file folders and name tags.

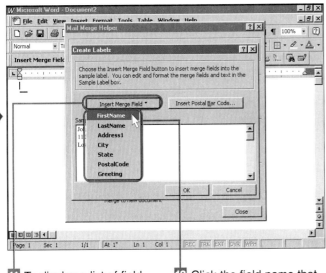

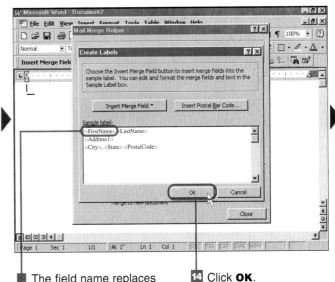

■11 To display a list of field names, click **Insert Merge Field**.

Note: The field names that appear depend on the field names you specified when you created the data source.

■12 Click the field name that corresponds to the text you selected in step **10**.

■ The field name replaces the text you selected.

■13 Repeat steps **10** to **12** for all the text you want to change in each label.

■14 Click **OK**.

CONTINUED

USING MAIL MERGE TO PRINT LABELS

After you merge the
labels and the data
source, you can print
the labels.

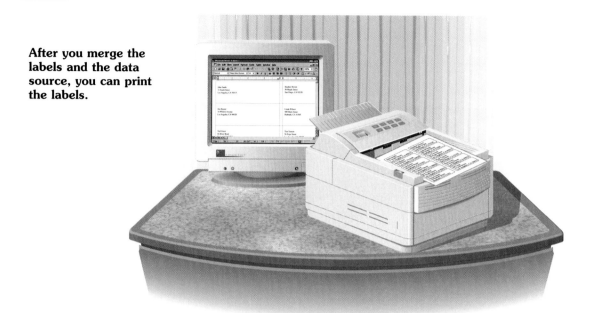

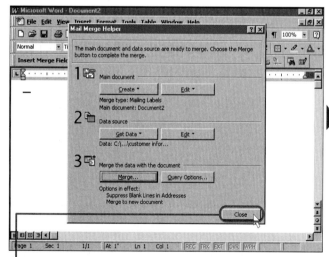

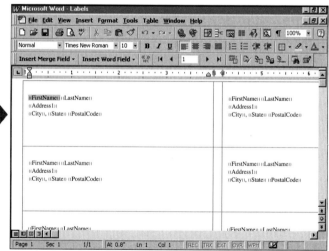

15 To close the Mail
Merge Helper dialog
box, click **Close**.

■ The labels appear,
displaying the field
names you selected.

16 Save the document.
To save a document,
refer to page 22.

*Note: In this example, the
document was named* **Labels**.

Should I save the merged labels?

To conserve hard drive space, do not save the merged labels. You can easily recreate the merged labels at any time. To do so, open the label document you saved in step **16** on page 274. Then perform step **17** below.

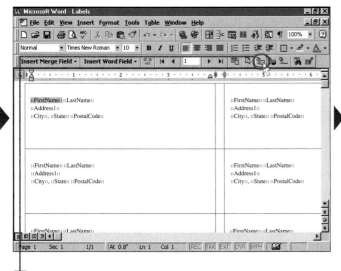

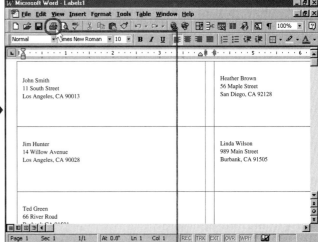

17 To merge the labels and the data source, click 🔲.

■ Word creates a personalized label for each customer.

18 To print the labels, click 🖨.

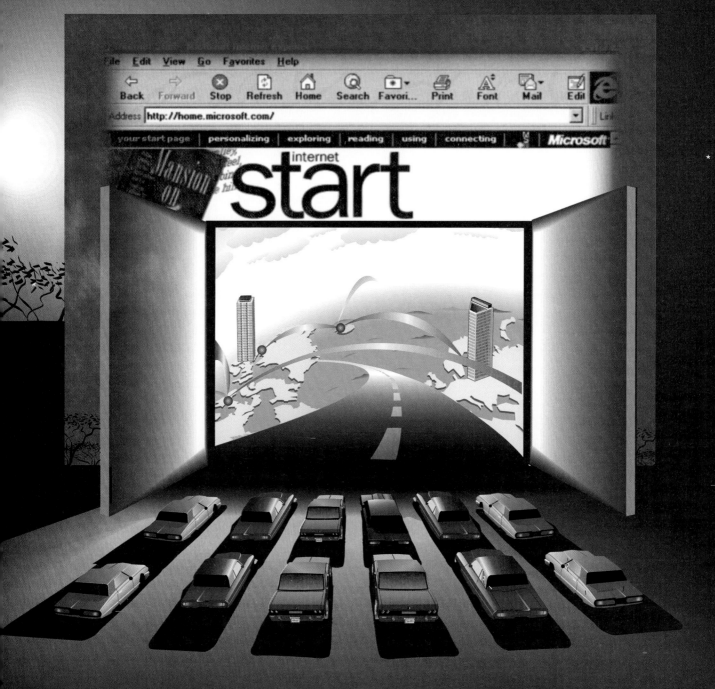

CHAPTER 16

Word and the Internet

How can Word help me take advantage of the Internet? Learn how to create hyperlinks, use the Favorites feature, save a document as a Web page and more.

CREATE A HYPERLINK

A hyperlink is a word or phrase that connects one document to another document. You can easily create a hyperlink in your document.

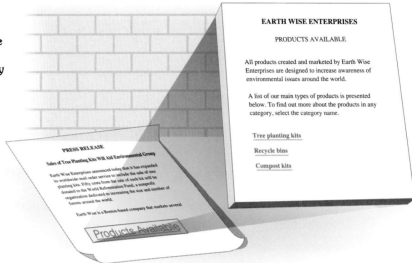

■ CREATE A HYPERLINK

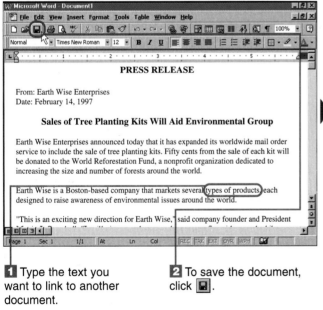

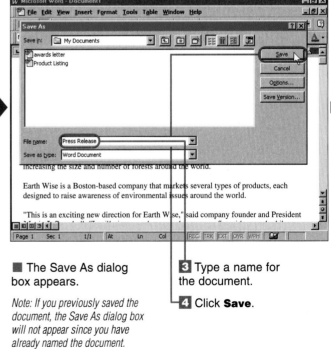

1 Type the text you want to link to another document.

2 To save the document, click 📄.

■ The Save As dialog box appears.

Note: If you previously saved the document, the Save As dialog box will not appear since you have already named the document.

3 Type a name for the document.

4 Click **Save**.

Where can a hyperlink take me?

You can create a hyperlink that takes you to another document on your computer, network, corporate intranet or the Internet.

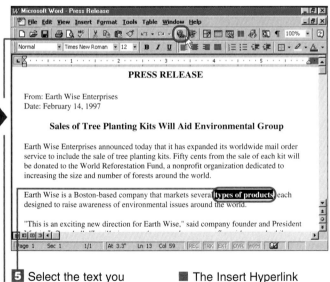

5 Select the text you typed in step **1**. To select text, refer to page 12.

6 Click 🔗.

■ The Insert Hyperlink dialog box appears.

7 To link the text to a document on your computer or network, click **Browse**.

■ To link the text to a Web page, type the address of the Web page (example: http://www.maran.com). Then skip to step **10** on page 280.

CONTINUED

CREATE A HYPERLINK

You can easily see hyperlinks in a document. Hyperlinks appear underlined and in color.

EARTH WISE ENTERPRISES
We care about the environment.

All products created and marketed by Earth Wise Enterprises are designed to increase awareness of environmental issues around the world.

A list of our main types of products is presented below. To find out more about the products in any category, select the category name.

Tree planting kits

Recycle bins

Compost kits

■ **CREATE A HYPERLINK** (CONTINUED)

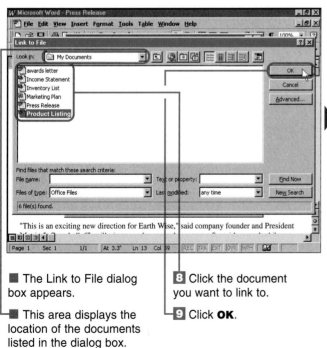

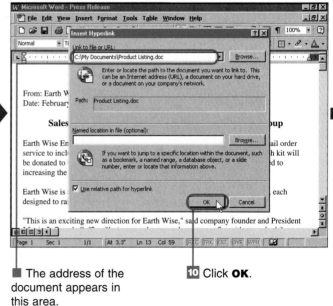

■ The Link to File dialog box appears.

■ This area displays the location of the documents listed in the dialog box.

8 Click the document you want to link to.

9 Click **OK**.

■ The address of the document appears in this area.

10 Click **OK**.

Can Word automatically create hyperlinks for me?

When you type the address of a document located on a network or the Internet, Word automatically changes the address to a hyperlink.

http://www.maran.com

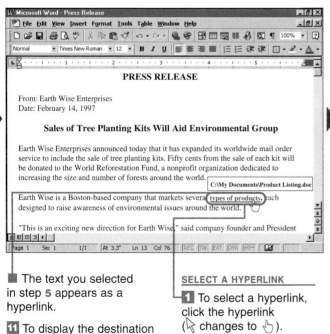

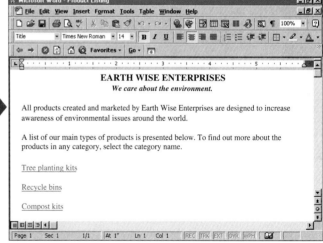

■ The text you selected in step **5** appears as a hyperlink.

11 To display the destination address of the hyperlink, position the mouse ⬚ over the hyperlink (⬚ changes to 🖑). After a few seconds, the address appears.

SELECT A HYPERLINK

1 To select a hyperlink, click the hyperlink (⬚ changes to 🖑).

■ The document connected to the hyperlink appears.

■ If the hyperlink is connected to a Web page, your Web browser opens and displays the Web page.

DISPLAY THE WEB TOOLBAR

You can display the Web toolbar to help you browse through documents containing hyperlinks.

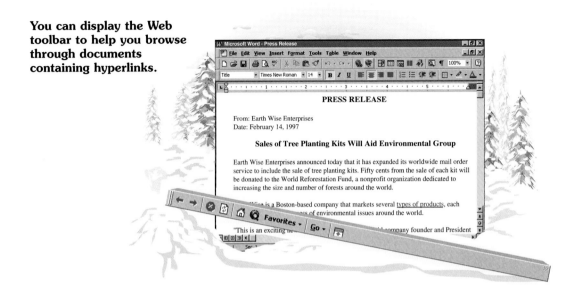

■ DISPLAY THE WEB TOOLBAR

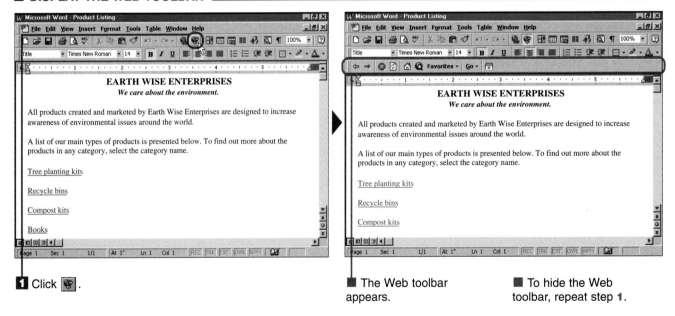

1 Click 🌐 .

■ The Web toolbar appears.

■ To hide the Web toolbar, repeat step **1**.

MOVE BETWEEN DOCUMENTS

When you view documents by selecting hyperlinks, Word keeps track of all the documents you have viewed. You can easily move back and forth between these documents.

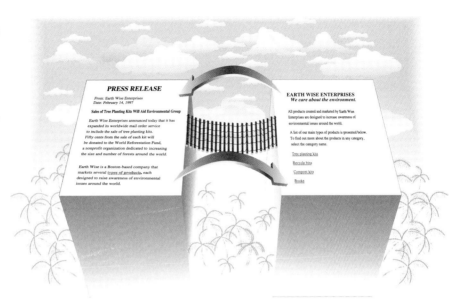

■ MOVE BETWEEN DOCUMENTS

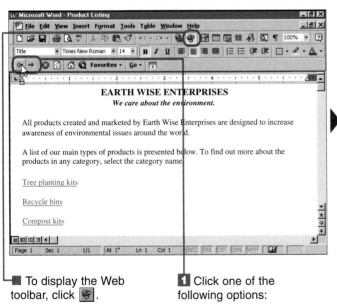

■ To display the Web toolbar, click 🌐.

1 Click one of the following options:

⇦ Move back

⇨ Move forward

■ The document you selected appears.

OPEN A DOCUMENT

You can quickly open
a document that is on
your computer, network,
corporate intranet or
the Internet.

■ OPEN A DOCUMENT

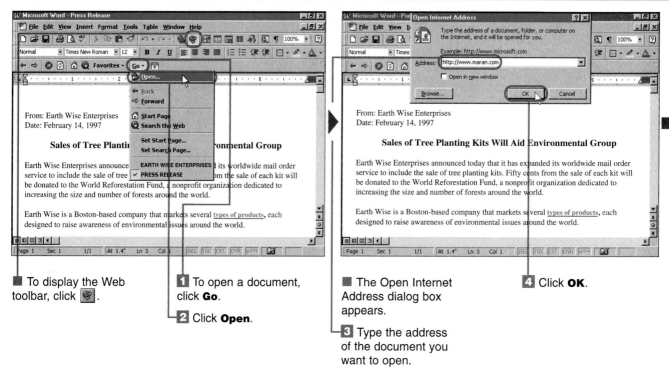

■ To display the Web
toolbar, click [image].

1 To open a document,
click **Go**.

2 Click **Open**.

■ The Open Internet
Address dialog box
appears.

3 Type the address
of the document you
want to open.

4 Click **OK**.

If a Web page is taking a long time to appear, you can stop the transfer of information.

■ STOP THE CONNECTION ■

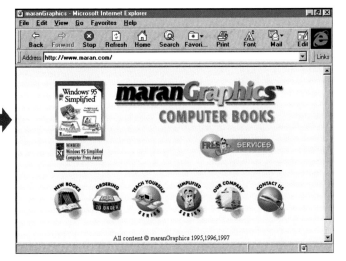

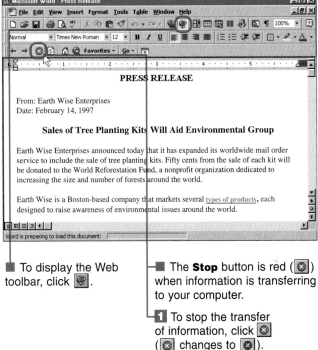

■ The document appears.

■ If you typed a Web page address in step **3**, your Web browser opens and displays the Web page.

■ To display the Web toolbar, click 🌐.

■ The **Stop** button is red (⊗) when information is transferring to your computer.

1 To stop the transfer of information, click ⊗ (⊗ changes to ⊗).

DISPLAY THE START PAGE

The start page is the first page that appears when you start a Web browser.

The start page includes instructions and hyperlinks that let you quickly connect to interesting documents.

■ DISPLAY THE START PAGE

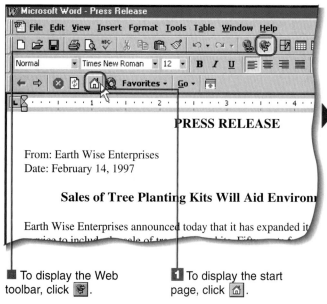

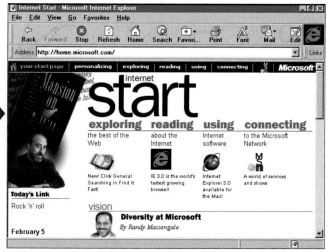

■ To display the Web toolbar, click 🐲.

1 To display the start page, click 🏠.

■ Your Web browser opens and displays the start page.

■ This page is automatically set as your start page.

286

The search page helps
you find information of
interest.

DISPLAY THE SEARCH PAGE

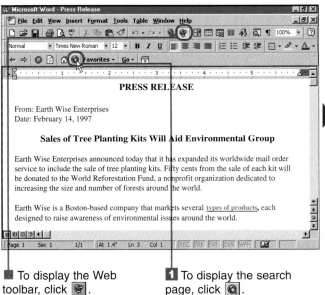

■ To display the Web
toolbar, click 🌐.

1 To display the search
page, click 🔍.

■ Your Web browser
opens and displays the
search page.

■ This page is automatically
set as your search page.

ADD A DOCUMENT TO FAVORITES

You can add documents
you frequently use to the
Favorites folder. This lets
you quickly open these
documents at any time.

■ ADD A DOCUMENT TO FAVORITES

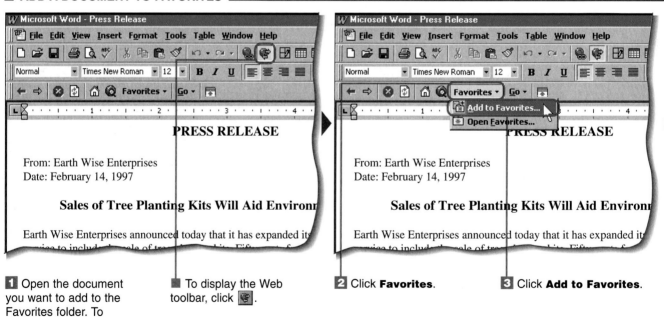

1 Open the document
you want to add to the
Favorites folder. To
open a document,
refer to page 30.

■ To display the Web
toolbar, click 📖.

2 Click **Favorites**.

3 Click **Add to Favorites**.

288

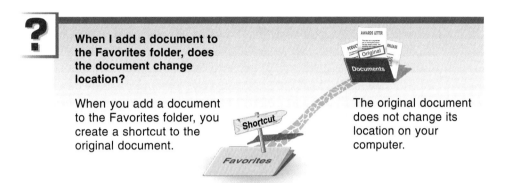

When I add a document to the Favorites folder, does the document change location?

When you add a document to the Favorites folder, you create a shortcut to the original document.

The original document does not change its location on your computer.

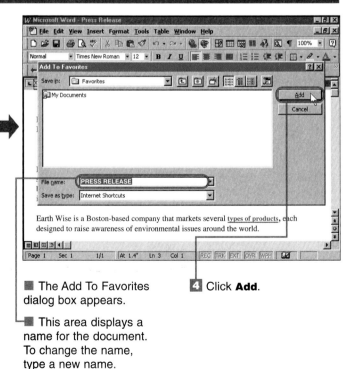

■ The Add To Favorites dialog box appears.

■ This area displays a name for the document. To change the name, type a new name.

◢ Click **Add**.

■ **OPEN A DOCUMENT IN FAVORITES**

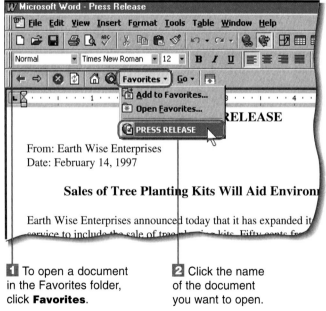

◢ To open a document in the Favorites folder, click **Favorites**.

◢ Click the name of the document you want to open.

LANIMATE TEXT IN A DOCUMENT

You can make text in your document move or flash. Animation effects help emphasize text in a document that will appear on the company intranet or the Web.

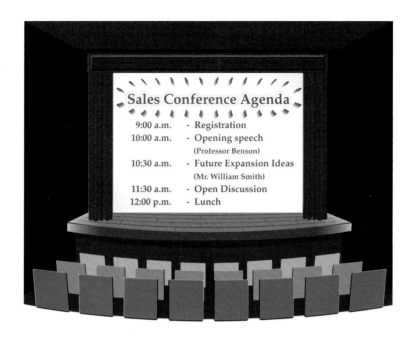

■ ANIMATE TEXT IN A DOCUMENT

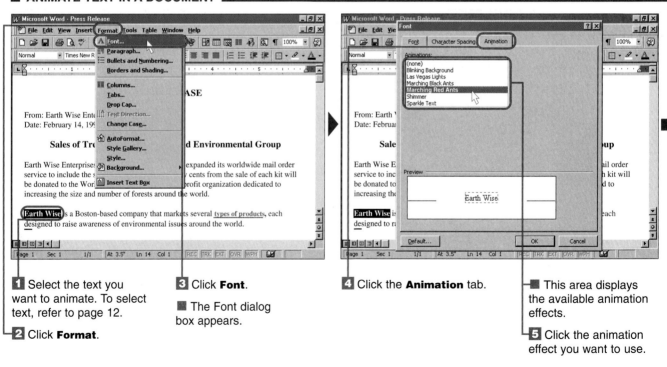

1 Select the text you want to animate. To select text, refer to page 12.

2 Click **Format**.

3 Click **Font**.

■ The Font dialog box appears.

4 Click the **Animation** tab.

■ This area displays the available animation effects.

5 Click the animation effect you want to use.

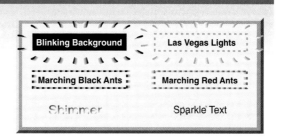

?

What types of animation effects does Word offer?

Word offers several animation effects that you can use to draw attention to text in your document.

Blinking Background   Las Vegas Lights

Marching Black Ants   Marching Red Ants

Shimmer   Sparkle Text

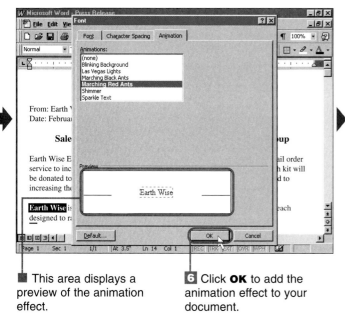

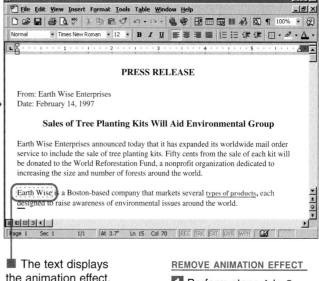

■ This area displays a preview of the animation effect.

6 Click **OK** to add the animation effect to your document.

■ The text displays the animation effect.

Note: Animation effects will not appear when you print the document. For information on printing, refer to page 180.

REMOVE ANIMATION EFFECT

1 Perform steps **1** to **6**, selecting **(none)** in step **5**.

ADD A BACKGROUND TO A DOCUMENT

You can add a background
to a document you want
to place on the company
intranet or the Web.
Word offers many
textures and colors
you can choose from.

■ ADD A BACKGROUND TO A DOCUMENT

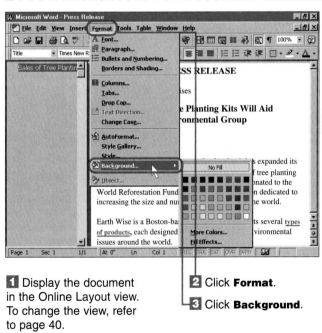

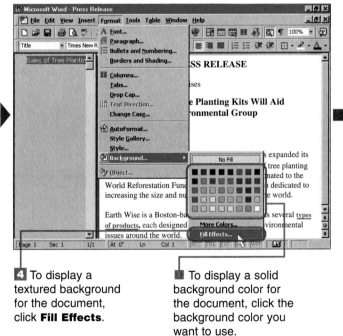

1 Display the document
in the Online Layout view.
To change the view, refer
to page 40.

*Note: Word does not display
backgrounds in the Normal view.*

2 Click **Format**.

3 Click **Background**.

4 To display a
textured background
for the document,
click **Fill Effects**.

■ To display a solid
background color for
the document, click the
background color you
want to use.

■ The Fill Effects dialog
box appears.

How can I make the text in my document easier to read?

Make sure you select background and text colors that work well together. For example, red text on a blue background can be difficult to read. To change the color of text in your document, refer to page 96.

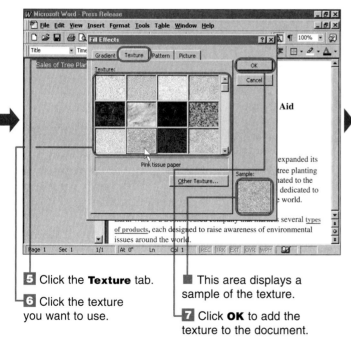

5 Click the **Texture** tab.

6 Click the texture you want to use.

■ This area displays a sample of the texture.

7 Click **OK** to add the texture to the document.

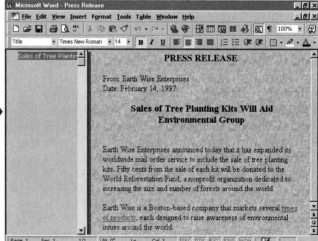

■ The document displays the new background.

Note: The background will not appear when you print the document. For information on printing, refer to page 180.

SAVE A DOCUMENT AS A WEB PAGE

You can save a document as a Web page. This lets you place the document on the company intranet or the Web.

■ SAVE A DOCUMENT AS A WEB PAGE

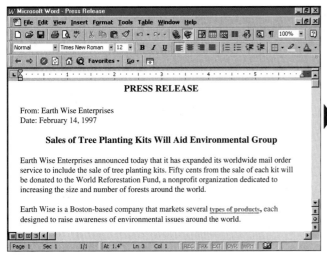

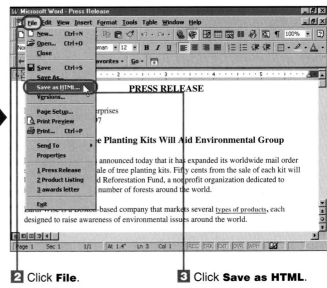

1 Open the document you want to save as a Web page. To open a document, refer to page 30.

2 Click **File**.

3 Click **Save as HTML**.

*Note: If the **Save as HTML** command is not available, you need to add the Web Page Authoring (HTML) component from the Microsoft Word or Microsoft Office CD-ROM disc.*

Can Word help me create a new Web page?

You can use a template or wizard to help you create a new Web page. Templates and wizards complete the layout and formatting of a document so you can concentrate on the content. For information on using templates and wizards, refer to page 234.

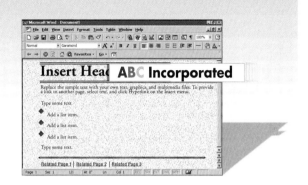

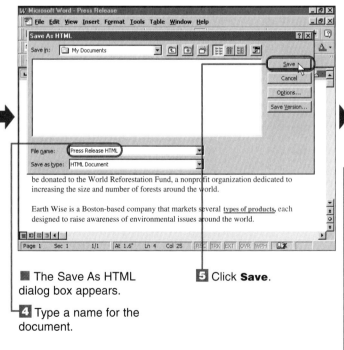

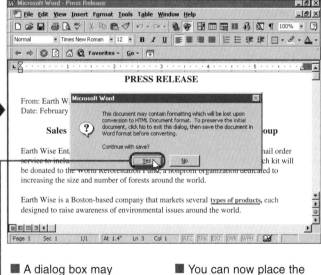

■ The Save As HTML dialog box appears.

4 Type a name for the document.

5 Click **Save**.

■ A dialog box may appear, warning you that your document may contain formatting that will be lost.

6 To save the document as a Web page, click **Yes**.

■ You can now place the document on a corporate intranet or the Web for others to view.

INDEX

A

align text, 93. *See also* indent; tabs
  in cells, 210
animate text in documents, 290-291
arrange open documents, 194
AutoCorrect, 73, 78-79
AutoFormat, Table, 214-215
AutoShapes, 218-219
AutoText, 80-83

B

background, add to documents, 292-293
blank lines
  delete, 53
  insert, 51
bold text, 92, 99
borders
  page, 150-151
  tables, 212-213
  text, 124-125
bottom margins, 153
breaks
  pages, 144-145
  sections, 146-147
browse through data sources, 261
bulleted lists, 122-123
buttons, display names, 17

C

cells in tables, defined, 203
center
  tabs, 116. *See also* tabs
  text, 93
    vertically, 148-149
change
  case of text, 56-57
  paper
    size, 156-157
    source, 188-189
  text direction, 211

changes
  save, 23
  undo, 53, 55
character styles, 169
characters. *See also* text
  count, 86
  delete, 52
  display nonprinting, 87
  insert, 50
  leader, 120-121
  spacing, 108-109
  special. *See* symbols
click, using mouse, 7
clip art, 220-221
close
  documents, 28
  Word, 29
color
  graphics, 228
  highlighted text, 97
  text, 96, 100
columns
  newspaper, 160-161
  in tables
    add, 207
    defined, 203
    delete, 208
    width, 203
comment
  add, 88-89
connection, stop, 285
control page breaks, 154-155
copy
  formats, 104-105
  text, 60-61
    between documents, 196-197
count words, 86
create
  drop cap, 128-129
  template, 236-237
  toolbar, new, 250-251
customize the toolbars, 244-249

INDEX

INDEX

INDEX